The *Witch Bottles* Compendium

Compendium

Discover the Power of Spell Jars While Understanding and Owning Your Magic

~

Including 100 Recipes for Love, Protection, Abundance Prosperity, and More!

PHOEBE ANDERSON

First Printing Edition, 2021

Printed in the United States of America

Available from Amazon.com and other retail outlets

PERFECTBOUND2.0

Published by Perfect Bound 2.0 Design and Writing © 2021 Perfect Bound 2.0

Thank You!

Thank you very much for taking the time to read this book. I hope it positively impacts your life in ways you can't even imagine.

If you have a minute to spare, I would really appreciate a few words on the site where you bought it.

Honest feedbacks help readers find the right book for their needs!

TABLE OF CONTENTS

~

INTRODUCTION

Witch bottles, also called spell jars, are little jars or bottles that store all of the power of a spell. This simple, tailored practice makes it easy to be creative and to adjust the energy in our life. Spell jars are one of my favorite things since they serve as a constant reminder of my objectives. I also admire them for their openness! Every time you look into them, you can see the layers of your labor. Witch bottles or spell jars may be used for almost any spell goal.

There is also something inherently beautiful about them that makes me feel they are pulling power from within myself as if the whole world is smiling at me, and when I'm close to them, I feel like I've just accomplished something. And that beauty can be physical, not just conceptual! That's why, every time I am about to buy a new spell jar, I just think immediately of all that I've accomplished so far.

But remember, everything in your spell will revolve around the concept of your intent. Your intent, as often happens in magic, should be:

* **Specific:** Concentrate on specific objectives (no wishing, no generalizing, no multi-purpose spells for 12 different things).
* **Achievable:** Make sure your objectives are realistic (no Dungeons & Dragons or Harry Potter fantasy stuff).
* **Ethical:** I won't tell you what is or isn't ethical, but you should think about your spiritual ethics and the repercussions of your acts.

Once you've decided on your goals, you may also start plannin¬g your jar spell, including everything you'll need to put in it to fulfill your goal.

In this thorough yet practical book, I will immerse you in the realm of craft and teach you that the more effort you put into developing and casting your own spell, the more successful the result will be. You'll also discover that presenting spells without first teaching the foundations, such as grounding, centering, casting a circle, and so on, is pointless—it won't work! I'll also offer the tools I've built over the years to help you understand yourself and tap into your inner strength. In addition, you'll find 80 different jar spells to help you attract desired energies into your life.

Be assured that I will not offer you specific rules to follow, but rather recommendations, because many of us have experienced witchcraft according to the code that we've set for ourselves.

WHAT DOES IT MEAN TO BE A WITCH?

Witches are feared, oppressed, and misunderstood. They are considered the source of every bad thing that goes wrong in reality. From plagues to natural disasters, all of these things are supposedly witches' doing. This is just one aspect of the witch stereotype that is commonly repeated in modern culture, with very little evidence to back it up.

Witches are the source of many of today's most popular beliefs, but what exactly does it mean to be a witch? There are some definitions out there, but the dictionary doesn't always offer satisfactory answers. That's because witchcraft is more than just casting spells or practicing magic. Being a witch entails being conscious of your own power. Be aware that you construct yourself and the environment in which you live and that you control the forces that shape your life—for better or worse—being in touch with that inner stream of creativity, magic, and intuition that runs naturally inside all of us but is unreachable to most people because it's buried so deep in the mind that it can't be seen, touched, or comprehended by the conscious mind.

It's possible that you don't always feel like a witch. But whether you realize it or not, that wicked witch is ready to emerge from deep inside you. It's hidden in the depths of your psyche!!

How do you get started? The simplest way is to find other women who are already practicing witchcraft and ask them for their advice. They will be able to give you specific instructions on how to continue down the path. They've experienced the power of witchcraft, not because they were born this way, but because they chose to embrace it.

What is the essence of witch training? A witch is someone who takes action to make the world a better place. She's not afraid of her anger because she knows that it's stronger than her fear. A witch knows that there are more powerful things in this world that are more important than what you look like or who your parents are. Witchcraft is more than just learning how to cast spells—it's learning how to think for yourself, trust the universe, and use your own magic to create something spectacular.

What does it make a witch different? The most important thing that separates witches from other women is their willingness to stand up for women as a whole and fight against those who try to put them down. A witch doesn't care about what you think because she knows that the only opinion that matters is her own. When it comes down to it, a witch is someone who has the courage to be herself and the wisdom to know what's best for her.

What is a witch's most incredible power? The greatest thing about witchcraft is that it gives women the tools they need to take control of their lives. It doesn't matter if you've been abused or beaten down by life; you still have the ability to be powerful and confident just like everyone else. That's why witchcraft isn't just something that you practice—it is something that will change your life completely.

What does witchcraft mean to me? Witchcraft is something that has always been around women but didn't get the respect it deserved until recently. It's an act of defiance against anyone who tries to put you down because it means that you say no to the world outside of yourself. A witch is someone who refuses to be defined by anyone or ANYTHING except for herself. It's an act of independence that will change your life in ways that you never imagined.

As a witch, you hold the power to manifest change, but you must respect free will no matter what. Trying to alter another person's free will can have grave consequences. Be careful when casting spells that include others, and be mindful of your intentions.

NON-MAGICAL BENEFITS FROM WITCHCRAFT

Here are some of the true advantages of practicing witchcraft in your everyday life.

* Grounding might calm you down when you're anxious.
* Creating a tangible memory of what you want in life with rituals and spells is a fantastic concept.
* You can stim (self-stimulate) using both crystals and anxiety stones.
* Certain herbs may really help to alleviate typical disease symptoms (but you cannot use them to cure illnesses).
* Meditation may help you with your visualization exercises, which is great for artists!
* Knowing about witchcraft may help you have an insight into different cultures' spiritual practices.
* Spell jars might assist you in remembering your objectives.
* If you believe in a god or deal with spirits, you may talk to them about your issues and get things off your chest.
* A ritual routine may assist you in creating or adhering to a routine, which can be good for your mental health.

Part 1

FOUNDAMENTALS

"The moment you doubt whether you can fly, you cease for ever to be able to do it." — J. M. Barrie, Peter Pan

Witching on a Budget

Preparing for your first year can be overwhelming. You'll need to obtain vital witchery instruments in addition to the spell materials. You may not have much money right now, but that should not stop you from learning about the world of witchcraft; it is more affordable than most people think. For example, most witch stores offer free shipping if over $25, and they often give discounts during one-time sales like Black Friday or Christmas. You can also find great deals online, such as through Amazon Prime for extra expedient shipments. Once you've collected all of your supplies, you can choose to help out a local online store and do some witchcraft shopping with the money you've saved.

Of course, purchasing all these items can really add up and be hard on your budget, but with a little thought, you may often discover everything you need right in your own home! I've listed the tools and supplies below that you will need to get started, along with some ideas for using items found around the home for some of them. Throughout the book, you will also see specific items listed for certain spells or rituals.

TOOLS

Wand - I believe that the finest wands (and believe me, I'm a big supporter of the exquisite, customized, hand-turned wands you can purchase) are simply wood rods that communicate to you on a personal basis. Go outdoors and choose a length of wood that you like for thickness, flexibility, and feel, attempt to figure out what kind of tree it came from, then consecrate as required. Going outside and finding your wand is the greatest way to create a connection with it! If a branch doesn't appeal to you, try something alternative, such as a long candle for a fiery witch or a wooden spoon for the kitchen witch.

Altar Cloth / Altar - For an altar cloth, use a bold color from a cloth napkin, tablecloth, or perhaps a scarf or shawl. Crates flipped on their ends or boxes (skip cardboard if you plan to use candles in the long term) make excellent altar bases, and you can even store all of your witching equipment in them.

Salt - It is a witch's must-have item! Salt, kept in a tiny bowl, container, or bag, is used in plenty of rituals and spells to protect, cleanse, consecrate, and reflect the element Earth. Table salt is good but kosher and sea salt are much better. A pinch of salt is frequently enough to purify or cleanse any objects or instruments on the road (at least for this witch!).

Athame / Ritual Knife - Many witches use a bowline, athame, or ritual knife to chop herbs, direct power, or perform rituals. A regular table knife or butter knife may be used, with the handle wrapped in thread or twine to match the color of your instrument (black for a "100% correct Wiccan" athame, for example, or white for a flexible Green Witch depiction of a working knife, for another instance).

Cauldron - Trust me, a cup will be enough. Choose a heat-resistant mug or an oil warmer that you prefer. If you have an oil warmer, you may utilize the oil storage area as a typical (although small) cauldron workspace warmed by the candle below.

Book of Shadows - Keeping track of your practice is a great (and popular!) idea. You can begin with a simple notebook or a journal. I like to use a ring binder to add and rearrange items as I need. And, I also use sheet protectors, which are great for protecting the pages from candle wax and other ritual dripping. Some modern witches use a digital version. A Book of Shadows pulled up on a smartphone is no less valid than a more classic notebook!

WITCHY SUPPLIES

Candles - Candles are not just for decorative purposes. They are used as an instrument in spells that enact changes, perform divinations, or protect against harm. They can be lit with spell-casting intent to affect energy work on all levels—earthly, emotional, mental, and spiritual—or with cleansing intent to remove negative energy from your space before doing magic elsewhere.

Candles are an integral part of even the most basic witchcraft. One of the prerequisites for being a witch is to have your own authentic, natural candle. When selecting candles for use in spells, it's essential to understand that different types are used for different purposes. It's also important to know that candles are never burned during magic rites. They are lit for divination purposes only.

White candles are used for protection and purification, as well as to represent the element of fire. They are also used to cleanse the psychic aura, banish negative energy, and protect against harm.

Lavender is used in protection, cleansing, and in healing spells. It is my personal favorite spell candle. It sets my intentions in motion—cleansing my space of negativity before I cast spells.

Green candles represent the element of earth and are used for protection, healing, and abundance spells. They are also used to give notice that you are doing magic. You can align the candle with your personal power center or with the north to call upon earth energies. When using green candles for healing magic, snuff out the wick after the candle is finished burning so that only the wax remains to be placed on a chakra or organ related to your condition.

Brown or red candles are used for love spells and increasing passion. They also correspond to the element of earth. Brown is a base color but can still be used to align with other colors associated with an emotion you wish to invoke in your spell work.

Yellow or gold candles are used for prosperity, fertility, healing, and the element of air. Yellow attracts wealth, which means it is also used in money spells. These two colors are also used for divinations by aligning with the north to raise power to determine what action will create the best results.

Blue or purple candles are associated with water and spirituality. Blue is aligned with the east (air) and west (water) sides of your space in magic rites to cast spells related to these elemental energies. Purple is aligned with the elements of magic in your space when it's in its correct place in relation to you during magic rites. Purple represents spirituality and wisdom; blue is associated with mental clarity and insight.

Black candles are used to banish, break bad habits, protect during travel, and eliminate energy that is detrimental to your spells. Black is an interesting color because it has the ability to absorb the energy around it. It is never aligned with any particular element in magic rites. When you choose a black spell candle for use in magic, be sure to place it so that the wick is positioned toward you while burning.

Crystals - Witches use crystals for a variety of purposes, but most often, it is to stimulate psychic powers, promote health, or ward off negativity and bad energy. Crystals are often associated with specific energies that they produce on their own when on the earth's surface, but they can also be imbued with certain properties through various tasks such as lighting candles near them or burning incense near them. They are used to add power to spells or keep bad spirits from affecting certain areas of your home. They are used in meditation and visualization to raise energy and pull it up through your chakras. They help you to open your third eye or crown chakra in order to obtain higher spiritual access. Some magical practitioners use them as a substitute for summoning a spirit to receive specific information from a spirit without opening a door between the two worlds.

Dry Herbs - It was believed that witches use plants and herbs for magic, but now many people are using dry herbs to make incense or for medicinal purposes. Many believe that there are magical properties created by combining different types of plants together to form an incense formula. Some believe these ingredients are used because they have specific healing properties or because they create a symbolic representation of the witch's desire or need.

Dry herbs and flowers offer all types of possibilities for the witch who wishes to use them in a positive way and can be used in a number of ways. For example, you may choose to use the herbs or flowers to create a spell or potion that will help you accomplish your goal. In addition, you may simply use the dry herbs by themselves to cleanse your body of negative energy. There are even some witches who believe that they can ground themselves by rubbing the dry herb between their palms.

Many witches believe that burning certain plants will attract certain spirits, most commonly spirits of nature. These types of events can be a way to celebrate a special occasion or holiday by showing gratitude for the natural world. When a witch does use herbs in a spell, they usually use an herb that they have either found or received from another person. Because of this, spells may look different depending on the type of herb used. For example, if you use a root, the spell could appear as if there was some kind of cleansing happening. In addition, if you were to dry an herb down before using it for a spell, the outcome could certainly change from the outcome you would expect from using fresh herbs.

Dry herbs and flowers can also be used in a healing spell or potion. For instance, if you wanted to place an enchantment on a plant so that it would grow faster, you could use the dry herb called basil to help speed up the growth of your plant. In addition, if you wanted to heal someone who was sick, you could create a potion with witch hazel and lavender. Since herbs such as rosemary and basil attract spirits of nature, it is said that they can also attract positive spirits such as angels. If you wish to invite positive energy into your life, then natural herbs may be just what you are looking for.

Herbs can also be used to cleanse your aura. You can simply place a few drops of essential oils on your palms and rub them together to cleanse the body of any negative energy. In addition, herbs can be scattered around a room to cleanse any negative energies that may linger in the area. An incense mixture made from natural herbs can also be used in order to do this.

Tarot Cards - The use of tarot in witchcraft is controversial but can be used in positive ways.

Many modern witches are turning to the cards for guidance on questions pertaining to their personal spiritual development or workplace dilemmas. It's crucial for witches who wish to use tarot cards in their practice to consult with a teacher before giving this type of reading.

In terms of spiritual development, tarot cards can be used as a way to help you figure out what kind of witch you are.

Past life card readings and those that focus on the future can be very helpful in the process.

Charms - The use of charms is a complicated subject within witchcraft. Many witches, especially those who practice some kind of polytheistic or pantheistic system, also use charms as a means to express their belief in a God or Goddess.

One common use would be for prayer practices. In this case, a witch would cast a spell or use a charm creating a magic formula, which can be spoken, sung or chanted, containing the intention that it will bring about some sort of change in her life or another person's life. However, this would be an informal way of asking for something to happen rather than petitioning for it. You will find plenty of examples of incantations, charms, and intentions in the spells gathered in this book.

Another everyday use of charms is for divination practices. This type of practice is often used by witches who practice one or all of the Goddess-based belief systems that many pagans today subscribe to. In this case, the witch would cast a charm on some object or person that she or he wishes to vision. Afterward, she will seek a vision from a deity in order to gain insight into what may come true.

Yet another use of the use charm is simply to bring about pleasure or happiness. For example, a witch may cast a use charm on another person's head to make them see the beauty in life, rather than the harshness they are always looking for. The theory behind this kind of practice is that if someone can be found happy, all will be well with them, henceforth others in their circle of influence.

As you can see, witches use charms to help people, not to curse or cast hexes upon people, as you might have seen depicted in movies or on television.

TOOLS BY SPELL TYPE

Generally speaking, magical tools are wildly versatile. They can be used to represent intangible concepts or deities, to direct our energy, and to perform somewhat mundane tasks like cutting herbs or producing ash. In some spells, however, tools have very specific uses. And these uses vary from spell to spell. Some tools appear most often with certain types of spells. These tools are usually limited to stones or herbs, but they can also be certain types of ritual clothing or items as well as items that only fit the theme of a specific spell. In this chapter, I will go over how certain tools perform special functions depending on the spell you cast and will touch on a few tools that only appear for certain types of spells.

Love Spells - Love spells are somewhat controversial in the magical community. If done incorrectly, they are considered a sort of magical roofie. They take away someone's free will and cause them to act in a way they do not want to act. Even when done right—when the spell only calls for a certain kind of energy to enter your life in a romantic capacity—some magic users still find them distasteful. Before learning how specific tools are used in love spells, you should consider your stance on the spells themselves. From there, you can decide if this section is for you.

For those who approve of love spells, I feel I must clarify that I do not condone love spells cast on specific people. All of the tools in this section are intended for spells that do not target a person. Instead, these tools should be used to call a certain kind of energy into your life so that it can connect with you on a romantic or sexual level. At no point should you use this information to get a specific person to see you romantically or sexually.

With that rule firmly in place, we can move on to the tools themselves. As I said at the beginning of the chapter, tools serve many purposes. When you are casting a love spell, the tools take on some very unique purposes. If your magic is influenced by Wiccan practices, you can use your wand or ceremonial knife to represent a male partner while your chalice can represent a female partner. Using any combination of these two items can symbolize you and your partner joining together in a relationship. And, if you are polyamorous, you can use more than two.

Roses are also very common in love spells. Many spell sachets geared toward finding love will combine rose petals and rose quartz with sweet-smelling herbs and a few other trinkets. These are then placed under the hopeful lover's bed or carried in their pocket until they find the love they are looking for. As with the color pink, red roses are seen as a sign of romantic love in many countries, which is why they are used in spells like these.

Indeed, most spell bags for love spells are red or pink. The color also appears as the thread color in spell braids or the thread that bundles together herbs that may be hung around a hopeful lover's door. Some people may also incorporate lace or silk, as these are very tactile fabrics often found in lingerie and other clothing designed with romance in mind.

Moon Spells - Any spell that relies on the timing and energy of the moon is a moon spell. Given that the spells rely so heavily on our nearest celestial neighbor, it makes sense that most of the tools and items used in these spells would either display or represent the moon. That is to say, witches who predominantly practice moon magic will usually have ritual knives, chalices, and other tools that all bear the image of the moon.

As with love spells, specific stones appear more often in moon spells than they do anywhere else. Moonstone—also known as hecatolite—and opals are found in many moon spells. Both of them are usually predominantly white, as the moon appears in the sky, but bear a rainbow-like sheen when looked at from certain angles. This sheen is said to represent the energy of the moon.

Many witches, particularly those influenced by Wicca, see the moon as a source of female energy. And, for this reason, statues of goddesses are also more common in moon spells. So, the connection of the moon to female energy is not set-in-stone. As was valid with correspondence charts, you should always go with what feels right to you when it comes to the moon's energy.

Common colors in moon spells include very, very light blues—which also relate to the moon's color or its aura—and very dark blues. Very dark blues are more representative of the night sky, but they are an excellent backdrop for the brilliant stones mentioned above.

Many moon spells also focus on the use of moon water, which is basically any water that has been charged with the energy of the moon. This is usually done by putting the water in a clear glass container and then leaving this container in direct moonlight for a given length of time. The exact length of time varies based on the witch as well as the purpose of the moon water. Moon water can charge in the moonlight for as little one night or as long as one entire lunar cycle, which is nearly a full month.

Some moon water is charged during very specific phases of the moon. Full moon water is usually used for protective spells, fertility spells, and spells to ease menstrual pain. Water from the new moon is used for banishing spells, cleansing spells, and more aggressive protection spells than full moon water can produce. Witches who rely on moon magic will often charge a great deal of moon water all at once and then save it for use throughout the rest of the lunar cycle.

Your intention is what makes most tools effective for magic working. Without the guidance of your energy, the energy of spells will not know where to go or why it should be following the direction of your tools. If a spell is a car, then the energy you raise is the gas you put into it, and your intention is the steering wheel. It is your best—and really, your only—option when you want to steer the energy around you or the spell it is powering. This is just as true when charging moon water as it is with any other spell.

Nature Spells - For some witches, all spells are nature spells. Their energy is rooted in nature and the majority of their magical practice is rooted in a religion that honors the earth as a deity in and of itself. When you are this heavily immersed in nature, all of your tools bear nature energy and are for nature spells.

If nature is only part of your practice, however, you can do a few things to align yourself with natural energies more closely. This will be particularly helpful if you are trying to get your garden to grow better, learn something about the land on which your home is situated, or if you want to try and influence the weather in any way. Nature magic is also suitable for bringing out the nutrients in food, protecting your pets, and working larger spells with other witches to protect the wider natural world.

Choosing items made of wood or natural clay might not be enough, of course. If you choose a wand or cup made from a rare or frequently exploited wood, such as mahogany, you are not going to get a positive reaction from the natural energy you are trying to work with. You would have better luck using a stick from your backyard as a wand. Quite literally, as it would have a stronger connection to you and could be gathered without harming the trees in any way.

You can just as easily connect the rest of your tools to the natural world as well. Stones and herbs are already closely connected to the natural world, of course. But if you get your stones from a quarry that is open to the public, you will have a much more intense connection to them. The same thing will happen if you have something of a green thumb and can grow your own herbs. They will grow in soil that is protected by your magic and can then be harvested with a dedicated harvesting knife (in some practices, these are referred to as bolines). All of this creates a connection between you and the herbs so that they are even more effective when used in your spells.

Kitchen witches—witches who infuse their food and drinks with magic—will find this particularly useful. Handling their herbs from seed or cutting to the cooking pot allows them to connect with the plant's magic from the very beginning. So, when they go to add the plants to their cooking, the magical addition is even stronger.

If you can grow your own herbs, make sure you charge all of the gardening tools you use. Everything from your gloves to your watering can to the hose you use can be charged to infuse magic into the green growing things around you. You can also infuse fresh energy into the plants every time you settle in to tend them. This incorporates meditation as a sort of magical tool, which is something I cover in the final chapter of this book.

Now that we've covered many of the tools needed to get started, let's dive into some of the things you'll need to know how to do before you begin casting your spells, like building an altar, casting a circle, charging, grounding and centering, and cleansing.

TRUSTED SUPPLIERS

If you are a witch on a budget, like me, then you may be searching for witchcraft supplies that are affordable and that you can trust. It is easy to find scammers nowadays, so; I thought it would be good to share my favorite (trusted) shops.

* **Original Botanica - NY** | https://www.originalbotanica.com/
2486-88 Webster Avenue in the Bronx, New York

Family-owned and operated since 1959, Original Botanica is well-stocked and an excellent source for spiritual house cleaners, candles, and oils. They also offer free shipping on orders over $95 and consultations and readings (of course, in-store only). I recently bought Florida Water Cologne from them, and the water is so unique and very powerful. Anytime I'm feeling negative, I immediately spray this, and I'm feeling refreshed and optimistic!

* **Old World Witchery – Etsy**

This Etsy shop is known for its intricate blends of ritual incense and herbs. You can also pick up a couple of healing crystals while you're at it. I browsed Etsy for weeks looking for a few things to add to my apothecary, and all of the kits I found included so much that I didn't need. Old Word Witchery offers a customizable option of dry herbs, incenses, gums, and resins. The prices are accessible, and overall, I've always found it a good deal. Only once, I had an issue with delivery due to USPS, it took over a month, but everything was packed well, labeled, and exactly as ordered, plus an additional herb, which was a welcomed surprise.

* **Catland Books – NY** | https://www.catlandbooks.com/
987 Flushing Avenue in Brooklyn, New York

This Brooklyn-based occult store is a go-to pick for its selection of old and new witchcraft-related books, as well as tarot cards. Online you can also get unique preferences like the Dionysian wand, perfect to finish off an altar!

Building an Altar

The most common tool among witches is not the wand. It is, in fact, the altar.

Consider your altar to be a specific spot inside your "holy space" where you may concentrate, meditate, and gather energy for your spells. This holy place is also shielded from negative energies, ensuring that you are safe and gathering good energy. There should be no resemblance to a micro workplace in the design. Instead, it should resemble a spot where someone might sit in solitude while praying or contemplating. Constructing and designing a basic altar is straightforward, and its usage is defined by the spells that are performed. Most importantly, it must be useful + it must reflect who you are and your views + it must be built to assist you in achieving your objectives.

Selecting a spot in your house that feels the nicest is an intuitive approach for deciding where to place your altar. The more engaged, spiritually connected, and joyous you feel in the room, the better it is. It doesn't matter how big or little your altar is—it might be a teeny-tiny space or a complete room. It's in really utilizing your altar that the magic happens! A witch's altar can come in many forms and sizes. Some witches prefer to create their altars on wall-mounted shelves. Very useful for witches whose cats like to get involved! Others opt for whole tables dedicated to magical and religious purposes. Of course, both options work best for witches who are "out" and very open about their practice with anyone who may walk into their home. Not all witches fit this description. And, as such, their altars are often very different.

Witches who want a more discreet altar may opt for a miniature one, usually built inside a box. Some are even the size of a mint tin and intended to serve only as a focal point for the witch's power during spells or as a place for her to commune with her deities.

Others might use a table that they can take apart, such as the kind sold at most hardware stores. They store this table, in pieces, under their bed or in a closet. Their tools and altar decorations are stored in another box or scattered around their room, used as décor, until they need to put them to magical use. When the time comes the witch assembles her table and sets up her altar. Although this option is quite a bit of work, it does provide a little more energy to the spell or ritual since the witch expended the energy necessary to set everything up and then take everything down when she is done.

Yet another altar option is a digital altar. This modern take on the witch's altar can only serve as a focal point and a place to commune with deities or spirits, of course. But many modern witches keep blogs that serve as a form of altar. Or they create static images that they change and update the way other witches would change the décor on their altar. Their tools are typically stored near the computer where the witch keeps her digital altar and brought out when it is time to work magic.

You now have the groundwork of what makes a good altar. It is not so much the material it is made from but rather how well it serves your magical practice. But what about the tools that go on your altar or the decorations I mentioned earlier? Both of these topics might seem a bit confusing to new witches. Rest assured; we will cover them both together.

As a witch's altar is a personal reflection of her practice, the exact tools and decorations will vary. The spells being cast, and the witch's own reflection of her practice decide the usage of a basic altar, which is actually fairly easy to create and decorate. You may adorn your altar with anything you wish... Allow your imagination to go wild while decorating your altar, but avoid using too many synthetic materials! The tools and embellishments used will differ.

Witches usually have a ritual knife of some kind or a wand, both of which are used to help direct the flow of the witch's energy. These knives or wands—to direct her energy, a witch could use either—can be made of any material. Some witches choose to make their own while others prefer store-bought.

Many practitioners also keep a chalice or cauldron on their altar to hold water. In certain magical practices, such as Wicca, the chalice represents the female divine, and the water within represents the life source from which we all emerge. Other practices, however, use the chalice strictly as a drinking vessel so that the witch can toast or cheer the spirits and deities she works with or worships.

Decorations are a little trickier. Some witches ascribe to the Wiccan Wheel of the Year and decorate their altar according to the season and the nearest religious holiday on the Wheel. Others arrange and decorate their altars to honor specific religious figures or spirits. For these witches, the seasons are not so much a call to change the appearance of their altar but a reminder to keep it fresh and clean. And then some witches do not decorate their altar at all. They forego flowers, stones, images, or growing things to keep a clean work surface. As with choosing the best type of altar, each witch must decide how to decorate her altar. Or whether she wants to decorate it at all. For those that practice more with the 4 elements, it is typical to place depictions of each element in each direction on the altar. Earth is housed in the north. Air is located in the east. South encompasses fire. Water is directed to the West.

Outdoor altars are great for dealing with volatile elements (like a campfire or digging in the ground), as well as fairy and deity magic.

An altar is used to help you focus on your spells with energy and items that are used in rituals. Your altar should inspire you and always be carefully maintained. As a workspace, it should be large enough for you to conduct your spiritual workings.

When selecting altar items, choose objects that have meaning to you, don't clutter your altar with unnecessary things as this may decrease your energy levels. Simply select items that reflect you and your path. If you want to find the perfect altar for your witchy rituals, here are some tips that can help you choose one that's right for you.

* Know your needs. If your goal is to create an altar for devotional purposes, select altars with small shelves and drawers to store items like holy cards or statues of saints. If ritual magic is more your thing, then be sure to get an altar with lots of open space on top where spells and other ingredients can be stored during the ceremonies.
* Depending on the spell you are going to do, you can customize your altar with various objects and tools. Choose the colors of the candles, statuettes, charms, incense, stones, herbs, and jewelry to align with the energy you are trying to project or evoke.
* Think about its location in relation to doors and windows. Your altar should be on a level floor where it can be viewed from all angles. If it is on a higher floor, the altar will not be as visible to people who are coming or going from the room. Some spells require the altar to be next to a window on the full moon, so it's a good idea to have a temporary altar that you can mount and dismount.

A couple of very important things to do before setting up your sacred space:

1. Clean the entire room where your altar will be. Make sure the area is free of clutter and dirt. Having a clean space will help you focus on your spell. You can use a home cleaning ritual or simply dissolve sea salt in water and wipe the walls, ceiling, and floor with a clean cloth.
2. Remember to cleanse your sacred space within the circle. First, consecrate your tools with pure, positive energy from your heart. Or charge a little water with your energy and then use that water to clean your altar.

Casting a Circle

You do not have to use your altarpiece to cast your circle. You may be out in the woods when you need to cast and may be far away from your altar. You might also just utilize your altar to store your magical tools between casting and will not need to involve it in your Wicca work. However, you may find that you feel more grounded in your practices if you start by connecting with the energy of your altar before casting your circle.

Why do you cast a circle, and what does it even mean? When you invoke the energies all around you and connect your energy to the spiritual plane, you need to have an opening and closing of intention and protection. Casting is almost like a meditation to get you engaged with your work and get you ready to cast your spell.

Establish the amount of space you will need for your ritual or spell; for one person, stretch out your arms and use a circle big enough to encompass you. If movement is needed for the ritual or spell, use more space and, for groups or ceremonies including altars, ensure that all the space required is covered by the circle.

Have all the items you need for the ceremony at hand before you cast the circle. During a spell or ritual, you will require focus and do not need to be interrupted by searching for items you need. It is also best to avoid breaking the circle once it is cast.

Cleanse the area, literally. Clean, vacuum, and dust. Cleanse the area ritually by using a broom, burning incense in the room, or sprinkling salt or saltwater around the space. Importantly, whichever method you choose, visualize negative energy dispersing from the sacred space as you carry out your ritual.

With the area cleansed, you can now cast your circle. Simply trace the area of the circle itself out in a way that best suits you. Many people use a wand or simply their hand to 'draw' the circle. You merely need to point whatever tool you use at the ground and define the circle as you go. To cast the circle, you should walk clockwise (sunwise in Wiccan and witchcraft traditions), starting at the eastern point of the circle. Visualize energy, power, and protection as you make your transit. You may complete one circuit or several. Three, six, and nine times are considered appropriate as these numbers have powerful spiritual vibrations. Many people like to call out the four directions as they reach them (north, south, east, and west), but again, this is down to preference.

Once you have cast the circle, you can proceed with the ritual or spell. Avoid breaking the circle during the ceremony if at all possible. If you must, visualize a door opening in the circle, imagine this opening and closing as you leave and, once you have returned, sealing up completely.

At the end of your ceremony, you should disperse or open the circle. This is generally part of the end of a ritual or spell, and we will cover opening the circle as we look at those techniques.

The meaning of casting a circle in your preparation is also to align you with the four directions and the four elements. Each way you travel is represented by your circle, and each element of the life spark is represented to connect you to your full purpose and potential. It is a meaningful acknowledgment of your journey when you cast a circle that brings into focus things that will help you succeed on your path: the directions and the elements.

Remember to create a space that feels healthy and balanced for you while you practice. It is best to do it away from where others will interrupt or disturb you. The following steps will help you cast your circle of intention and protection.

If you are working near your altar and you want to include it in your ritual, you can begin by lighting candles on the altar and lighting your smudge stick to cleanse the energy of the altar and your body.

Facing the north, say the following words:

"I call upon the energy of the north. Welcome to this circle of light. And so it is."

Facing the east, say the following words:

"I call upon the energy of the east. Welcome to this circle of light. And so, it is."

Facing the south, say the following words:

"I call upon the energy of the south. Welcome to this circle of light. And so, it is."

Facing the west, say the following words:

"I call upon the energy of the west. Welcome to this circle of light. And so, it is."

CLOSING YOUR CIRCLE

Closing your circle is as simple as opening it. All you have to do is pay respect and gratitude to the elements and the directions. You may want to face each direction again to ask the directions to comfort you on your path as you allow your spell to take effect.

You can also connect with the elements you have in your space and carefully return them to their altar space as a way of creating closure with them. Here are a few steps to help you close your circle, as you opened it:

Thank each element by addressing it directly. For example...

Sprinkle salt or soil into your hands and rub them together, letting the salt/soil fall away naturally and saying:

"Thank you to the Earth that grounds me."

Snuff out the smudge stick and say the following words:

"Thank you to the air that blows me forward on my journey."

Blow out the candle and then say the following:

"Thank you for the fire the lights my way."

Dip your fingers in water and flick on your altar or your face, saying the following:

"Thank you to the water that cleanses and purifies."

THE MEANING OF THE CIRCLE

The circle is not a temporary sacred space; it is a temporary temple—a formal place where a witch may work and worship in safety. Remember that:

~

Witches consider the entire world, material and nonmaterial, to possess inherent sacred energy.

Witches consider themselves to be containers of a spark of divine energy.

~

These two beliefs working together mean that we can formally designate any area as sacred at any time, as the Divine within us recognizes the holiness inherent in the physical location through the ceremony of raising a circle.

On a physical level, you create a circle by walking around a perimeter of your intended workspace, often three times. Simply walking in a circle three times defines the circle's space in your mind, but it does not create the energy barrier Wiccans understand the circle to be. The energy used for channeling comes mainly from the earth, to which you ground yourself before raising the circle, but also partially from within the caster, as you must guide that energy with your will.

Baby witches understand the concept of walking the circle, but it takes a while before they channel energy with confidence as they raise one. Casting a circle begins as an act of faith, to an extent; you believe the circle is there. Over time you will realize that the energy within the designated space is very different from the energy outside it. This concept is something you learn—for example, if you have to cut a door in your circle to fetch something you've forgotten, you'll feel the difference between the energy within the circle and beyond it. More proof comes when you've done a strenuous and taxing ritual and dismantle the circle to be met with a cool breeze and relaxed energy, a direct contrast to the heat and higher vibrations you felt while the circle was still up.

There's nothing wrong with casting and dismantling circles just for practice. A circle is a step within a larger formal sequence, nothing more. Don't feel obliged to include the invocations and ritual workings that you normally do in a formal ritual. Instead of raising it with the intention for it to be a temple space, practice raising it to refine your circle-management skills. Before you experiment with the more advanced techniques of circle dissolution, make sure you ground and dismiss all the extra energy inside your circle.

Charging

Movies and books would have us believe that charms and amulets must be beautiful pieces of jewelry or intricate carvings. But that is far from the truth. You can enchant everything from your laptop to your shoes to your sunglasses, depending on the need you are trying to fill. If you want to use a piece of jewelry or a unique stone, you're more than welcome to. But you are only truly limited in your enchantment targets by your energy levels, your creativity, and the time you have to spend on your magical workings.

The exact method you use to enchant your chosen objects will vary depending on your energy source and the item you are trying to enchant. You can hardly enchant a car the same way you would your shoes. And you are not likely to work your magic on them for the same purposes. Because of this, I can only give a general idea of how you can enchant an object and suggestions for what purposes you can enchant them for.

Generally speaking, it is easier to cast an enchantment than a spell. Enchantments take less energy and, usually, less preparation. Some witches choose to enhance their enchantment by working their magic during a particular phase of the moon or time of day. These are usually related to a deity they work with since the moon's phase and the time of day hold specific meanings in certain cultures and for certain deities.

Using your own preferences and connections, you can choose when to cast this enchantment. Whenever you choose to cast it and whatever you decide to cast it on, you need only to follow this general template and guide your energy as instructed below.

When you are ready to cast the enchantment itself, close your eyes and gather your energy from your core and the immediate area around you. Visualize it swirling around your hands and up your arms. Now draw your tendril back into yourself and guide the source's energy along with it, through your body and to your hands.

Take a few moments to ensure that the source's energy is flowing into both hands. You may find that your energy flows more strongly into one of your hands than the other. This is likely because you have a dominant hand, as most people do. Your dominant hand will likely be the one guiding most of the energy when you work with your magic, but you want to make sure both hands have access to the energy you need.

Once the energy is more or less balanced, pick up the object you want to enchant. Or, if the object is too large, place both hands against its surface. Imagine your energy flowing over the surface of the object until you have surrounded it completely. There should even be a little bit of your energy between your hands and the surface of the object. While you do this, hold your intent in your mind. Repeat it over and over like a chant, or visualize the object working the way you want it to without fail.

When it is surrounded completely, push your energy into the object. Watch the energy sink under the surface until you can feel it within the core of the object itself. If the item is particularly large or made of a material that does not easily take energy, you can repeat this process a few times. This will ensure that your energy has sunk into the targeted object. If you want to check how much energy has been absorbed, remove your hands and shake them off to rid yourself of any excess energy. Then open your eyes and touch the object. You should feel a faint tingle or shiver. The strength of this sensation will depend on how much energy you have instilled in your targeted object.

There are very few limits on the ways you can enchant your objects. No, you can't enchant your shoes so that they make you fly. But you can give them a magical boost that kicks in when you are running late for your bus and need a little bit more speed. And you might not be able to turn invisible. But you can enchant your favorite sweater to help unwanted eyes slip away from you when you are out walking.

Some enchantments are more popular than others. You can spell your glasses to ward away smudges and water droplets. Bags can be enchanted so that they don't collect crumbs or they stop eating pens. Shoes can be made to stay cleaner for longer, and garments can be encouraged to repel food stains and missing buttons.

Most modern people rely heavily on technology, which is another place where enchantments can come in handy. You can coax a stronger or more consistent signal from your wi-fi router. Or you can spell your phone so that you always remember to check if it is on wi-fi or cellular data. You can also use your magic to help your phone filter spam calls or blocked numbers more effectively. And you can charm your phone screen so that it is less prone to cracking, chipping, or scratching.

As you can see, enchantments are suitable for everyday annoyances. Missing buttons and smudged glasses aren't going to ruin your day. But they can make a good day turn sour and a bad day worse. Enchantments can solve plenty of small problems or help avoid them altogether. But for slightly larger everyday issues, you will want to turn to spells.

CHARGING METHODS

Often times before casting a spell, you will want to charge certain items that will be used in the spell. This is just a way of infusing extra energy into the objects. There are dozens of methods for doing this. You have to find the way that suits both yourself and your intent, and it'll all come easily.

No matter which method you use, the energy of your own focused intention is the key to the process.

1. Visualize the outcome you're seeking when you charge your ritual tools and magical ingredients.
2. Tactile connection—holding the object in your hands or placing your fingers on it while it rests on a surface—is a good way to transfer your power to it.
3. Speaking words of intention can really help you hone your focus, so come up with some words that express your desire here.

Here there are just a few to start.

Moonlight - Place your item so it's illuminated by the moon. Charge it overnight if you wish!

Crystal - If you have a pre-charged or cleansed crystal (and you can cleanse one by running it under cold water), you can place it on top of or next to the item to charge it. Crystals can be used as "charging batteries" in this way!

Earth - Lay your item out on fresh earth or on the ground. Press your hands into it and feel the Earth lend its power to, and draw excess energies from, the item.

Personal Power - Place your hands together over or against the item, drawing power from the ground, air, or your usual power source, then directing it into the item.

Candle - Light a candle with intent by, or on, the item. The candle is usually left to burn out.

Fire - This method is used when an item is to be consumed, such as a sigil on paper. Non-flammable items can also come into brief contact with fire (such as a candle flame) for charging.

GROUNDING AND CENTERING

Grounding and centering are among the most important things a witch ought to know as they can help you to stabilize your energy, draw energy from the Earth, and bring yourself into a positive state of being. Doing so is a good practice when preparing for a ritual or a spell; often, I see newer witches who have yet to learn this skill experiencing unnecessarily intense backlash from their spell work. It can also be performed anytime you feel upset and need a pick-me-up. Now, let's see both techniques in more detail.

GROUNDING

You have probably heard of meditation. You might have participated in meditation practice in a retreat of some kind or a yoga class. But even if you have meditated before, there is a chance you might not have been instructed in the art of grounding yourself. And it is even less likely that you have been trained on how grounding your energy affects your magical practice. Although the process is similar to standard meditation, the focus is a little bit different. When you ground for magical purposes, your focus is not so much on emptying your mind as on taking stock of your energy levels and their content. Later on, in the centering section, you will learn how to control where your energy goes. Typically, a witch grounds for one of two reasons. The first reason is to anchor herself before a magical work, which I will cover in more depth later in this chapter. However, she may also ground herself when she feels that she has taken on too much negative energy and she needs to get rid of some of it. In these cases, the act of grounding can be done by itself. And though it might take a fair amount of time when you are first starting, over time, you will find that you can ground and release negative energy in a matter of minutes without much direct thought. You do not have to master grounding this thoroughly before you move on to other meditative tools, of course. But it does help keep you free of negative influences and makes it safer for you to cast spells or do divination on the fly without raising as many protective wards.

Before you begin any sort of energy work—which is another term for meditative practices and other ways by which you learn to control your energy—you need to raise your protective wards. When you are first starting with energy work, you are very vulnerable. Over time you will find that you are less vulnerable when grounded than you are at other times. But in the beginning, opening up your energy like this will leave you vulnerable. So, for now, it is best to do this behind the safety of a protective circle or other similar wards.

Once your wards are raised, you will want to sit in a comfortable position. You can lay down, but you run the risk of falling asleep if you try to ground while lying down, at least the first few times. So, settle yourself in a comfortable sitting position and close your eyes. When you have gotten comfortable, check in with your body. By this, I mean that you should locate sources of stress and try to release them.

Stress most commonly gathers at the corners of the eyes and across your forehead as well as in your jaw and cheeks. If you find that you are frowning slightly or clenching your jaw, actively work to let go of that stress. From there, you can move on to other high-tension areas such as your back or your shoulders. The one place that you want to keep tension, however, is in your core. Maintaining good posture is a small form of self-support and self-care that can make meditation of all types much more enjoyable. If you find tension in your core, just make sure that it is serving the purpose of supporting the muscles in your back and maintaining good posture. You will probably have to check in with your tension levels several times throughout your grounding practice, especially when you are new to the exercise. Trying new things can cause tension, even if only a little bit. So, as you work through the grounding process, you should periodically check in and ensure that you are being gentle with yourself as you ground your energy.

After you release all of your unnecessary tension, it is time to begin the actual process of grounding your energy. With your eyes still closed, imagine a thick root emerging from the base of your spine. You can also imagine a network of roots extending down from the places where your body is in contact with the floor if that makes you more comfortable. Whichever you choose, make sure you bury the roots deep into the soil. Imagine a strong wind trying to knock you over. If the wind fails to move you, even a little bit, the roots are deep enough.

Once you are firmly rooted, turn your attention to your energy. Find a place on your physical body or in your mind where you feel content. If you focus your mental imagery on that area long enough, a specific color will start to form in your mind. This is the color of your energy. When you have this color in mind, turn your attention to the rest of your body and your mind. Look for discolored spots in your energy. You will likely find them in physical places where you feel sick or mental places where negative thoughts dwell. Discolored energy is a sign that negative energy has taken over that location.

Take your time and identify as many spots of discolored energy as you can. Then, starting from the top and working your way down, visualize the discolored spots flowing from their current location down to the roots you sank into the earth. The energy might resist leaving as you push it down through the roots, as negative energy likes to latch onto something and not let it go. But do not give up. Push the energy down the roots over and over until every last bit of it has passed out of your root system and into the earth.

The earth will take this energy and cleanse it, then return the cleansed energy to the universe so that it can be put to fresh use. In this way, negative energies are given a second chance to make a more positive impact in the world.

Once you have released all of that negative energy, you will find that you either feel drained or feel like there are empty spots in your energy field. Addressing this issue is the final step in grounding. After releasing all the negative energy, you can draw fresh neutral energy from a few sources. The most readily available source is the earth that you have rooted yourself into. In addition to cleansing negative energy, the earth stores a lot of neutral potential energy. And this is something you can put to use so that you do not feel so drained and do not have empty spots in your energy field.

Generally speaking, grounding is a very good thing. It can help keep a witch balanced, no matter what they are going through or what spells they are performing. But grounding can also bring up things that people try to ignore in their minds, particularly when they go to turn out negative energy. If this happens to you, know that it is normal. It is part of what witches call shadow work, which is a vital part of any in-depth magical practice. I cover shadow work in greater detail in the last section of this chapter.

CENTERING

Grounding and centering are usually referenced together. But they are two separate practices with two distinct functions. That being said, they are complementary and work very well when used together. If you choose to use these processes together, you should always ground first, as this will give you a stronger foundation to work from. Once you are rooted, you will have a much easier time controlling where your energy goes. However, if you choose to center without grounding, you just have to make sure that you are careful not to unbalance yourself by releasing or spending too much energy at once.

As with grounding, you will find that you develop your preferred visualization methods as you get comfortable with the process. To begin with, however, I recommend the visualization that makes up the rest of this section. It is the centering visualization that I started with, and it is very simple while being wonderfully effective.

Centering, in general, is the act of evaluating where your energy is going and ensuring that you approve of all your energetic commitments. If you do not, you release some of the commitments as part of the centering process, then center your remaining energy in your core so that you feel more balanced. Before you get to this stage, however, you should raise your wards. Just like with your grounding practice, centering will eventually make you less vulnerable. But at the very beginning, this level of visualization work will open your energy up quite a bit. So, make sure you set your wards before you dive into the visualization aspect of centering.

The visualization exercise for this process is very simple. When you did your grounding exercise, you created a mental image of yourself that you used when you formed your energetic roots. You can use that same mental image of yourself for your centering exercise, or you can create a new one.

When your field of vision contains a mental image of your whole self, slowly spread a sense of awareness out around your body. This sense should reveal all the strands of energy that extend out from you. These strands represent all the energetic commitments you make. Some of these commitments will be obvious, like your connections to friends, family, and your work life. Others may surprise you, such as the level of energy you spend on gossip or worrying about misplacing your phone. We all spend our energy in countless different places. Centering helps us bring some of that energy back home.

Each person views the strands of their energetic commitments differently. For some people, it is the same color as the rest of their energy. These lines might all be the same thickness or vary in size depending on the amount of energy that flows down any given connection. Other people see the connections as a different energetic color since it is not their energy alone but is instead their energy connected with something else.

A third common visual representation of energetic commitments is for each commitment to appear as a different kind of connection. Some may appear as chains, particularly those connections you cannot cut but are not fond of. Others might appear as tinsel, twinkle lights, or ribbons. Each connection will bear its unique appearance based on the person or thing it is connected to and how you feel about them.

However your connections appear, take your time exploring them. Pay attention to whether or not they look different based on how you feel or if more connections go in one direction than in another. Once you are confident that you have highlighted the vast majority of your energetic connections, begin to go through them one by one. Decide if you are comfortable maintaining those connections. If you are, you also need to make sure that you are pleased with the level of energy you are putting into them.

Some unwanted connections can be akin to leaving leeches on your skin. They take from you and give nothing back, leaving you a little weaker with each passing day until you do not have the energy to complete the things that you want to complete.

When you find connections that you do not want to keep, you have a few options to choose from. The first of these is that you disconnect the energetic connection immediately. In order for this to fully work, some connections will require real-world or mundane actions, and you will have to make a mental note to take care of these after you are done centering. But, while you are still engaged in the meditative process, you can cut off the energetic connection as a first step in severing the connection altogether.

If you find several connections that you want to sever, you can gather them into a bundle and go through them all at the same time. You will still have to disconnect them one by one to ensure that you get back as much of your energy as possible. But rather than disconnecting one energy commitment and then refocusing your attention on evaluating the next connection, you can go through all of the connections and then lock your focus in on the process of disconnecting those you no longer need.

When you are ready to disconnect energetic commitments, you need to remember that you are doing so as an act of compassion for yourself rather than an act of punishment for whatever the energy is connected to. Framing the process in this manner will keep the energy at a neutral or positive level and prevent negative energy from attaching to you or the recently severed connection.

As you break the connection with whoever or whatever your energy was going to, envision the energy rolling back into your core like a tape measure or a length of ribbon being rolled back onto the spool. If you are still grounded, you may want to feed the energy down into the earth and draw up fresh energy to replace it. This is particularly true if the person or thing you were connected to was toxic, whether to you specifically or in a general sense.

It is best to cut all unwanted and unnecessary connections as soon as possible. But, of course, there are times when it is not possible for one reason or another. In these cases, you can leave the connections in place while putting a throttle on them. This will act as a sort of energy break so that you do not devote more energy than strictly necessary to these connections.

Energy throttles are also a good idea for connections that you do want to keep, regardless of how you feel about them. Just because you keep a connection does not mean that you should pour unlimited energy into it. In these cases, an energy throttle can help you maintain a better sense of balance.

When you have gone through all of your energetic connections and sorted those you want from those you do not wish to maintain, it is time to tend the remaining connections. Energetic connections, like any collection of growing things, need to be maintained. Nature maintains her gardens quite well. But when humans become involved, we take the burden of tending on ourselves. And our energetic connections are no different. So, take the time in this meditative practice to make sure all your energetic connections are healthy.

Checking the health of your energetic connections is something you should probably do more regularly than you do. Many witches make a point of checking in with these connections on a weekly or monthly basis. This prevents them from running into toxic situations that they are trapped in by pouring too much energy into them. It also ensures that they are not spending more energy than they have to give and running themselves ragged, sort of like an energetic budget check.

You might not be ready to commit to such frequent energy checks right away. Healthy energetic bonds should be a strong, pleasing color. The exact color and appearance may vary, as I already said. But it should be pleasing to you since it is your energy being expended. It should also look healthy without any breaks, cracks, or splinters. Finally, healthy energetic connections will not leave you feeling drained. You can adore the person or thing on the other end of an energetic connection. But if you are exhausted due to your connection with them, there is an imbalance you must correct.

If you have found any connections that you want to sever, doing so requires real-world action, now is the time to take it. Putting off the necessary real-world actions opens you to a new energetic connection that you then have to go back in and sever again.

⊷●●○⊖ ◉ ⊖○●●⊶

Methods of Spiritual Cleansing

Like our physical ones, our energy bodies need to be cleansed on a regular basis with care. According to the first rule of thermodynamics, energy cannot be generated or destroyed, but it may be altered. Cleansing is the process of transforming sluggish or bad energy into harmonized, positive energy.

SCRUBBING THE SOUL

Cleansing should be done at least once a week. The frequency is, of course, variable and based on your spiritual practice. Here's a list of situations when cleansing might be beneficial.

* When you feel imbalanced or "off"
* Before and after spell work
* After a fight
* When you're experiencing low vibrating emotions like despair, resentment, wrath, guilt, or humiliation
* When you're facing a lack of abundance

SPIRIT BY BODY

Your physical energy body is the first to need spiritual purification. This energy field is ruled by the element of Earth.

Cleansing with Smoke

This method includes using incense sticks, herb bundles, or a sensor to burn any plant. After the herbs are well-lit and regularly burning, wrap the item or person in the smoke, using whatever manner you want. To cleanse a room or a home, stroll through it and allow the smoke to sink into the air and fill the space. Imagine a white light enveloping the item, person, or location, transmuting any stagnant energy into balanced energy, having a window open during this procedure is typically a good idea.

Please remember that smudging, a ceremonial activity involving the burning of sage, is a closed practice exclusive to Native Americans. If we do not match their cultural background, it is critical to help preserve beautiful, distinct civilizations by politely keeping their practices out of our spiritual journey.

Music

This procedure is quite straightforward. Play any song you choose and let the vibrations take over your surroundings! Playing an instrument or making your own music earns you extra points. You can't go wrong as long as you've established the aim to cleanse. While you're at it, dance away the negative energy.

Cleansing Ritual

Just as a cleansing ritual can be used to protect against adverse and untoward spirits, these kinds of rituals can also be used to help remove similar energies from the body and to assist with the healing process. When you are worried about an illness or are not feeling great, then it can often be helpful to ensure that you are correctly cleansed of these kinds of auras.

YOU WILL NEED:

Incense to burn (sage, preferably)
A single candle (ideally silver or grey-colored)
A sprinkling of sea salt
A chalice or cup filled with water (tap water is fine)

Respectively, these items represent the four traditional elements: earth, air, fire, and water.

WHAT'S NEXT:

Place the candle in front of you in a quiet room and light the candle and the incense. Begin to settle into a meditative state and remember that the more relaxed you are, the more effective the spell becomes. For those who are feeling ill or under the weather, this can be a difficult step, but temporarily overcoming an illness can be rewarding in the long run. As soon as you are feeling relaxed enough, you can begin.

As the incense begins to smolder and the scent fills the room, cast your hand through the smoke several times. Allow the smoke to pass over your skin and notice the smell as it fills the room. As you are doing so, say the following words:

"With air I cleanse myself."

Next, hold your hand over the burning candle (not close enough to hurt, but close enough to feel the heat on your palm) and say:

"With the fire I cleanse myself."

As you say the words, begin to feel the negative energies and the illness burning and smoldering. Next, pick up a pinch of sea salt and rub it between your forefingers and thumb. Then rub the salt over the palm of each hand and say to yourself:

"With earth I cleanse myself."

Finally, dip your hands into the water and wash away the salt and the traces of sage incense. As you clean your hands, repeat these words:

"With water I cleanse myself."

As soon as this is complete, you can extinguish the candles with your still wet fingers and dry your hands.

A Spell for the Release of Negativity

If you are still encountering negative and harmful energies in your life, this can have an adverse effect on your health. In such situations, the most effective solution can sometimes be to simply ask the energies to leave. The power of wichcraft is such that not only will it help you identify these energies, but it will also grant you the power to dismiss them from your life properly. If this is the kind of situation in which you find yourself, then read on to discover the best way in which to deal with these issues.

To complete the exercise, you will need only a quiet room and a red candle.

Turn off all of the lights and place the candle directly in front of you. As it is lit, begin to enter into meditation. While you might normally close your eyes, you should instead leave them open and focus directly on the flame as it burns. As you consider the lit candle, focus on the power and the strength of fire as a general force. This is the kind of power that will grant you the ability to drive out the negativity.

Once you have become fixed on the idea of the fire, then you will need to say the following words out loud to the room:

"Any energy that no longer serves me,

please leave now.

Thank you for your presence.

Now I am sending you home."

How you say the words will matter. You will need to fill your voice with conviction, concentrating on the power of the fire before you and turning this power into the tone with which you will drive out the negativity.

Repeat the words, driving them out to the room at large. It can help to visualize the negativity being removed from your body, peeling away like a snake shedding its skin. This is the healing process made real, helping you find the right energy to heal yourself and drive out the unwanted energies.

As you proceed, you should feel yourself becoming lighter and lighter. Once this feeling begins to arrive, you may extinguish the candle and resume your day-to-day activities as you begin to heal.

THE OCEAN'S EMOTION

The astral, emotional, or dream body is the name given to this energy body. It is linked to the element of water and is the area where humans may receive and analyze psychic information.

Bathing

Making a bath spell/ritual bath is a peaceful and efficient way to cleanse the emotional body and take care of yourself. Carefully run the bath and infuse it with the purpose of cleansing your spiritual body profoundly. You may use whichever bath bombs, crystals, essential oils, or candles you'd like! To pull out and neutralize any bad energy, I recommend using sea salt. For comparable characteristics, apple cider vinegar is advised. The rest is all up to you.

Water of Blessing

Water that has been allocated for energy cleaning may be used in a variety of ways. Simply combine sea salt with water and bless it in any manner that corresponds with your spiritual practice to make this. Any herbs or crystals may be added to this water, but make sure they aren't harmed by water or salt before using them. Touch chakra points, brush door frames, or spray rooms with this.

MIND AT EASE

The mental body might be tough to cleanse, but if we spend the time to explore inside, we can gain insight and understanding. What we believe causes us to feel, which causes us to speak and do things. By simply understanding what we believe, and working to change it when necessary, we can begin to cleanse our minds and put them at ease. The element of Air is associated with the mental body.

Meditation on a Regular Basis

Developing a meditation practice is essential for being conscious and being receptive to Divine guidance. You may begin with 10 minutes every day and see what improvements you observe.

These are only a few techniques to cleanse your bodily, emotional, and mental energy bodies spiritually. Remember to be creative and have a good time!

Intuition in Witchcraft

Intuition is the ability to think about something without seeing it, hearing it, or experiencing it. It's an understanding that comes with instinct. When you feel your heart pounding and your mind racing, these are signs of intuition. Intuitive abilities can be a gift or a curse depending on who you ask. They have been glorified by ancient practitioners of witchcraft while being condemned by Christianity and other faiths alike.

In witchcraft, intuition is especially valued because it's often seen as a sign of being close to the divine. It also represents the ability to read energy so you can tell if someone is lying or misdirecting your attention in some way. Intuition can be very useful in many different areas of life, including relationships, career, and parenting.

When you're intuitive, you're able to see things others don't. It may seem like your gifts are strange or strange to others, but they work for you because they increase your insights into the world around you. Intuition is how you can see into people's minds or into the future. You may have felt it in how you experience what you see in a movie or on TV—this means that what was real for other people who saw the same thing wasn't necessarily real for you. For example, imagine watching an action movie where someone gets hit in the stomach over and over again with a baseball bat. You can probably imagine how painful that must be, but it might have been a fun movie scene for someone else who watched the movie.

In witchcraft, intuition is more than just a trick of the mind. It is an expression of your inner truth and your ability to follow your heart. The witch of old would have had more freedom to act on their intuition than our modern-day society with many rules restricting our actions.

By honing your intuition and psychic abilities, you'll improve your spell crafting, strengthen your witchcraft, and bring depth and richness to your daily life. Whatever strategy you take, you'll get puzzle parts that aren't linked. You can make sense of a jumble by understanding the issue and applying your instincts. Attempting to do magic without intuition is like trying to read a different language in which you are not proficient—you may pick up a few tidbits, but the likelihood of mistakes is quite high. If you're going to produce your own spells, bottles, pouches, and medicines, you'll need a lot of intuition. Throughout the book, I will provide ideas, advice, and tactics that I use to lead a more magical existence, such as how to tap into many different forms of energy, including the moon cycles, and utilize it to power your spell work (often drawn from many sources of the magical word). I recommend that you investigate various forms of psychic talents and identify your own elemental capabilities and weaknesses. And it will go a long way if you use genuine witchery to bring greater harmony and balance into your home, business, and circle.

LEARNING TO TRUST YOUR INTUITION

Listen to Your Body

Your body can give you signals about decisions you've made because it is connected directly to your intuition. Try to pay attention to your body, and stay tuned with how it is feeling. Try not to interpret too much at first, but rather, just be present and aware of how it feels.

However, if you are feeling anxious or unsure, it could be your intuition trying to warn you. In this case, you can use the traffic light method.

The traffic light method is an intuitive decision-making tool that begins with encouraging you to pause, which in itself makes a significant difference!

Once you are clear on your desired outcome, you can quickly judge whether what you are about to do, or choose, will be on the spectrum of green, amber, or red. Green – these make you feel good, take you towards your goal, bring you joy, happiness, and energy, and support your mind, body, goals, and life. Yellow/Amber – these include anything that, while not destructive, you need to proceed with caution and be clear on your boundaries. Red – these make you feel uncomfortable and are usually opposite what you really want.

Dreams

Dreams are a very useful way of paying attention to your intuition. This is because when you dream, your subconscious mind is running things rather than your conscious mind, which is constantly cluttered with other issues you have to deal with. Your mind wants to help you solve problems; it wants to help you figure out your future, so try to allow it. Dreams are generally not very straightforward, so it may be hard to interpret them.

Too Much Analyzing

The analytical mind is the enemy of intuition. If you are a person who needs to analyze every thought and action, then learning to trust your intuition is going to be difficult. Start with simple decisions, like going with the gut meal you wanted at a restaurant, where to go for your birthday celebration, what coffee to order at the cafe, what pants to wear to work, etc. Next, you can use your intuition for bigger decisions. For example, if your gut is telling you not to date someone, although you consciously feel they are very attractive or your parents will like them, try to trust that feeling and not go into thinking about why you have that feeling. An intuition is trying to steer you down a path that it already knows exists and is not making up new directions for you to follow.

Exercising Your Psychic Energy

Learning to trust your intuition is an important first step in the process of honing your psychic abilities. Doing this allows you to simply trust yourself and your thoughts without overanalyzing and constantly doubting as to whether or not you made the right decision. Trust yourself and the universe—what is meant to be will come.

This section is going to explore more exercises that will help you become more tuned with the right side of your brain; the side that is innately more creative and spiritual. You probably have heard of the two practices here, as they have become popularized by the movement of Mindfulness within the Western world. Meditation, and visualization, are spectacular tools that will literally help you open your mind in both a calming and observational manner and with a method that stimulates your imagination.

Meditation

Meditation is a relatively simple concept, although many people find its point confusing. The art of sitting, and just being, has been practiced for centuries for the people of Buddhist and Hindu cultures. Its benefits on mental health are astounding, and thus, it rapidly made its way over into the Western world. It isn't a practice that is only for monks; anyone can utilize it and feel its daily benefits.

The following exercise is a simple form of meditation and requires very little from you beyond your time:

1. Find a quiet place in your home where you know you won't be disturbed for 15-20 minutes.

2. You can choose to sit on a chair, with your feet flat on the floor or in the classic lotus position, folding your legs over one another. Some people also choose to lie down on the floor, or on their bed. Just make sure that you are not overly tired; you are not meant to fall asleep right now!

3. Once you are comfortable, begin breathing deeply, focusing on the fall and rise of your stomach.

4. Choose something to focus on for the duration of the meditation, whether it be soothing music you put on, the beat of your breathing, the ticking of a clock, etc.

5. When thoughts come up, which they inevitably will, don't be hard on yourself. Simply acknowledge that the thoughts are there, and then turn your attention back to whatever you choose to focus on for this meditation.

Some people think that they cannot meditate because their minds are too busy. They start the practice, and then scold themselves for not completely 'quieting' their mind. Meditation is an art form that takes years of practice, and the entire point is not to judge yourself for 'doing it wrong.' There is no way that meditating can be done wrong. There is not a certain formula or set of actions that guarantee an empty mind. Meditation is meant to bring attention to the thoughts about the past and future that you are having, and how often they overflow your mind, taking you out of the moment. It brings attention to the moment and asks you to gaze at it, as you gaze at a sunset or painting, without judgment or criticism. Judgment or criticism is going to happen because this is what most people are used to. Meditation offers another perspective on life and will significantly help you in tapping into your psychic abilities. So, carving out about 15 minutes a day should help you head in the right direction.

Visualization

Visualization is the direct opposite of meditation. In therapeutic terms, visualization is used to help people with severe anxiety and panic to think of a location or environment that helps them calm down. In terms of exercising your mind for the sake of psychic skills, it means applying your imagination still, but in a particular situation that relates to your life. This will help you explore further possibilities in your life outside what may have been closing you in as being more 'realistic' and 'practical.' Once you are able to do this for yourself, the concept of predicting the future and what occurs in it won't seem so out of reach.

1. Just like meditation, try to find a quiet, comfortable place to sit or lie down.

2. Before choosing to visualize, come to the situation with a particular problem in your life, a desire, a goal, etc. Choose one.

3. Since you have chosen one, go through it, and tell yourself a story about it. You are not meant to solve the problem here, should that be what you have chosen. However, you are meant to see all of the possibilities in any given situation.

4. Do this for about 15 minutes. This is your world, your story; there exist no limits.

5. That is all there is to it. Like meditation, if you take the time to do this every now and then, your brain is going to be strong and able to accept the energies of the future that are going to come to you.

Six Spiritual Truths

1. The Sun Is Medicine
2. Lucid Dreams and Manifestations Are Real
3. Healing Is an Everyday Process
4. Aureas and Energies Exist; Your Body Senses Them
5. Everything in this Universe Is Connected
6. The Moon Strengthens Your Psychic Ability

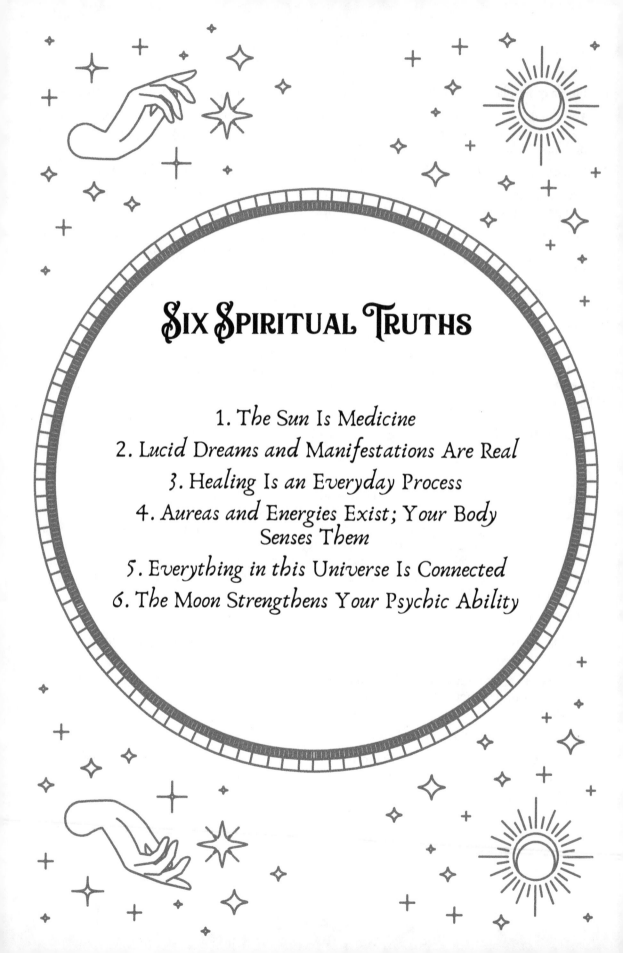

Psychic Ability Enhancement

The concept of a witch or even Wicca often connotes images of psychics that set up tents at carnivals and want to read your future. Although no one is here to debate whether or not any of those are legitimate, set yourself straight in acknowledging that Wiccans are not a part of that misinterpretation. What Wiccans and witches are, are people that are greatly in tuned with their intuition, and they follow that. Learning to sharpen these abilities is not about waking up and suddenly being able to read minds; it is about applying various practices that will enhance an ability all human beings were born with. We all have feelings about things that we cannot explain; we call those hunches or gut feelings. Wiccans believe that every person is born with some level of psychic ability, and it has been either encouraged or discouraged throughout their lifetime due to culture or particular upbringing.

The term ESP tries to cover every aspect of psychic abilities, such as clairvoyance, clairaudience, psychometry, telepathy, dowsing, precognition, scrying, and mediumship. These are not skills that you can easily tap into. Depending upon your upbringing, certain skills may be better than others are. It is going to take time to summon them to the surface when they have been pushed down for so long.

Your first step is for you to accept that you are capable of these things. You can start by reminding yourself every day with a statement such as: *"I am open and ready to receive information."* Begin researching, whether it be in other books or on the internet. You also need to know, that like most skills, you are not going to be good at every psychic skill. Try to figure out your strengths and what you feel you may have an affinity for. Most people are generally only extrasensory in one or two ways, so accept this and move forward, investigating your particular psychic skills.

WAYS TO ENHANCE YOUR MAGIC

Magic is a powerful force that can turn the tide of any battle. Nothing in this world comes without struggle, and while some creatures might seek to use magic for evil, witches are more than happy to use it for good.

Here are some great tips to enhance your magic to get you started on your journey to become an even more powerful witch:

1. Find out what your dominant element is so you can learn spells tailored to your abilities.

2. Expand beyond just witches and learn about other types of magicians like shamans and sorcerers!

3. Know the limitations of what you're trying to create through study or experimentation beforehand; not everything can be done with just magic.

4. Keep track of your spells so you can always recall them. It is helpful to have a notebook or place that is solely for spells that you need to remember.

5. Use whatever tools are available to help enhance your powers! Some of the most powerful spells rely on the use of specific tools such as ingredients and talismans.

6. Learn about different types of magical items and how they work! Knowing what these pieces do will certainly help you get more out of them!

ESSENTIAL OIL FOR ENHANCING PSYCHIC ABILITIES

Since before recorded history, oils have been used by priests, shamans, and healers. Oils are an especially vital component of rituals and other magical practices for witches. They correlate with the long-standing method of using the direct energy of nature to evoke change and transformation. They can be used in just about anything in magic, including incense, charms, altars, offerings, and ritual baths.

Essential oils hold a great deal of power as they hold the plant's magical energy which has been transformed into a liquid form. A huge component of the power of oils comes from their scent—which has a powerful impact on the mind. Oils open the pathways allowing us to have a direct connection from the natural physical world into the spiritual world.

Because they are often used in incense to evoke different scents, oils are powerful in rituals in helping us to focus on our intention and change our frame of mind. The scents are meant to help us shift from the mundane thoughts of our everyday lives into more profound thoughts—allowing us to develop further spiritual connections and help us achieve our goals. Using these oils can help us focus within ourselves, connect with our deities, and recognize our transformative powers. One particularly powerful combination of oils is myrrh and cedarwood—which awaken feelings that help us connect with the invisible forces in the universe.

SANDALWOOD For purifying, protecting, and it also has therapeutic properties. With this oil meditation, manifesting, astral projection, blessings, home cleansings, and letting go of the past are all possible. Negative energy is dispelled.

ROSEMARY can help you see visions, be more creative, and remember a prior life. It has the ability to eliminate negativity and is also used as a psychic stimulant. It also opens the third eye.

FRANKINCENSE is a powerful antiseptic. Protective, uplifting, cleansing, and balancing. It's great for connecting with your guides and for meditation. It promotes multidimensional awareness and enlightenment.

PEPPERMINT can be utilized to boost psychic awareness and spiritual vigor.

LAVENDER promotes dream recall and clairvoyance, and it aids in meditation. It also protects and purifies while opening the third eye.

CINNAMON stimulates visions, improves focus, and promotes healing and harmony. Connecting with guides is made easier with this tool.

JASMINE for inspiring, balancing, and sensual. Love, romance, and sex are attracted to it. Psychic dreams, astral projection, creativity, and visions are all stimulated. It encourages transcendence and compassion. It helps with meditation.

CRYSTALS FOR ENHANCING PSYCHIC ABILITIES

Psychics are those who have the ability to see, hear, feel, smell, taste, or have awareness beyond the physical world's bounds. Crystals can enhance this ability by possessing the energy inside and around a person, or by influencing a situation. Here are the types of crystals you can use different to amplify certain abilities:

Agate for communicating your intuitive needs.

Clear Quartz for cutting through the noise.

Rose Quartz for learning to love your inner voice.

Citrine for turning intuition into positive play.

Amethyst for crown chakra connections.

Selenite for aura cleansing and unravelling soul knots.

Lapis Lazuli for third eye opening.

Amazonite for emotional intelligence and intuition.

Celestite for cosmic thinking and angel realm connections.

Malachite for getting ready to rise.

Aventurine for overcoming obstacles and finding answers.

Fluorite for getting in flow and finetuning clear thinking.

Kyanite for cutting through illusion.

Obsidian for protection during a deep dive.

Sodalite for strengthening intuition and tarot reading.

Moonstone for a guiding light.

Labradorite for exploring your destiny.

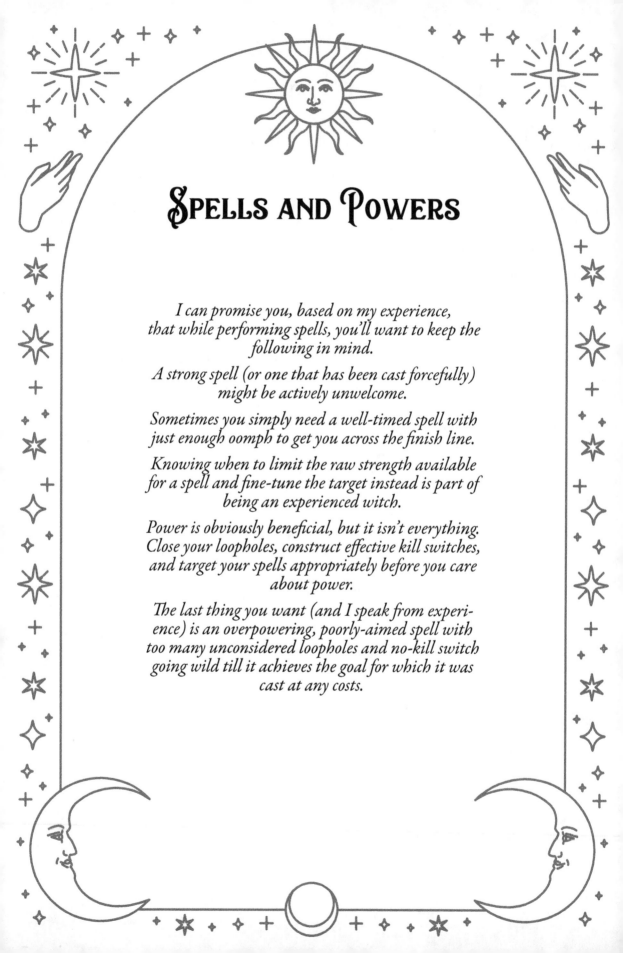

Spells and Powers

I can promise you, based on my experience, that while performing spells, you'll want to keep the following in mind.

A strong spell (or one that has been cast forcefully) might be actively unwelcome.

Sometimes you simply need a well-timed spell with just enough oomph to get you across the finish line.

Knowing when to limit the raw strength available for a spell and fine-tune the target instead is part of being an experienced witch.

Power is obviously beneficial, but it isn't everything. Close your loopholes, construct effective kill switches, and target your spells appropriately before you care about power.

The last thing you want (and I speak from experience) is an overpowering, poorly-aimed spell with too many unconsidered loopholes and no-kill switch going wild till it achieves the goal for which it was cast at any costs.

Moons and Spells

It's no secret that most individuals have a connection to Earth's natural satellite, regardless of whether or not they identify as witches. We all adore the moon, and learning how to harness the force of each moon phase may magnify your abilities and create some incredible spells. As a nocturnal witch, you use the powers of the night to perform your art. A lot of this kind of magic relies on pulling out the night's energy for use later. Here are a few instances... You may brew moon mater and preserve it to make tea later in the morning, or you can charge your letters with the energy of the night.

TAKE A LOOK AT THE MOONS IN A NUTSHELL!

Birch Moon is the 1st Moon (typically around mid to late January). The new Tree year is heralded by the moon of beginnings. It's perfect for new starts and initiations.

Rowan Moon is the 2nd Moon. The moon of astral travel and perception. Imbolc, and the Winter Solstice, are commemorated on this moon.

Ash Moon is the 3rd moon, and it is known as the moon of love and partnerships. Valentine's Day happens during this month.

Alder Moon is the 4th Moon. The moon of work. Excellent for self-governance and usefulness.

Willow Moon is the 5th Moon. The enchanting moon.

Hawthorn Moon is the 6th Moon. The disenchantment moon. It's useful for establishing boundaries and severing links.

Oak Moon is the 7th Moon. The moon of protection.

Holly Moon is the 8th Moon. The polarity moon. It's useful for reversing circumstances and encircling people. The first produce is also associated with this moon.

Hazel Moon is the 9th Moon. The moon of knowledge. It's useful for studying, researching, learning, and looking.

Vine Moon is the 10th moon, and known as the celebratory moon The second harvest is symbolized by this moon.

Ivy Moon, the 11th Moon, is the moon of strength. It is beneficial to one's health and personal concerns.

Reed Moon is the 12th Moon. The moon of home and hearth. It's good for house defense and magic. The 3rd harvest is symbolized by this moon (sometimes, this is Ivy moon).

Elder Moon is the 13th Moon. The moon of fulfillment.

FULL MOONS

The full moons of the year are referred to by different names and were initially used to keep track of the year and seasons. They are often utilized by farmers for crop management purposes. In magic, the full moon, based on the moon and the time of year, signifies the strong powers at hand and "flavors" and influences your spell.

WOLF MOON is January's full moon. Spells that strengthen and revitalize you, as well as self-care, prosperity, and healing spells, and also spirit work, are all influenced.

SNOW MOON February's full moon. Domestic magic, family magic, spells that help others, and psychic skills are all influenced.

WORM MOON is in March. Planning, preparation, and time-consuming rituals, wealth and healing magic, plus tech witchcraft are all influenced by this.

PINK MOON – April's full moon. It encourages development, green witchcraft, possibility, fresh beginnings, and relationship work via spells.

FLOWER MOON is May's full moon. Undertakings, foundations, spirituality, green/herbal witchcraft, and dealing with spirits are all influenced.

STRAWBERRY MOON is June's full moon. Friendship spells, love spells, magic that causes changes and reflection, and travel magic are all influenced by this.

THUNDER MOON is in July. Disciplining and purifying, higher-power magic, and storm/rain witchcraft are all influences.

STURGEON MOON is August's full moon. Magic that pays back to others that interacts with emotion, river, sea, and water witchcraft are all influences.

HARVEST MOON is September's full moon. Kitchen witchcraft cultivation, harvesting, and collecting debts, which some people consider a curse, are all influenced.

HUNTER'S MOON is the October full moon. Money, house, and protection spells are all affected, as is the quest for guidance and spirit work, as well as astral travel.

BEAVER MOON - November's full moon. Influences the house and hearth, as well as winter preparations, cosmic/celestial witchcraft, astrology, and revelation.

COLD MOON is December's full moon. Security spells, self-care spells, rejuvenation, and prosperity spells, and terminating and casting curses are all affected.

BLUE MOON occurs 1-2 times every year on average. Since the 12 complete moons do not split equally across the year, the month it occurs in shifts. If you're looking for a spell that promotes knowledge, healing, reasoning, and researching, look no further.

HARNESS THE POWER OF THE MOON

The night of the full moon is known for its beauty, its healing properties, its fantastic powerful energy, and its magic. There are many rituals and beliefs in various cultures and religions on the use of moon energy.

I believe the full moon is a time for healing, a time for recharging your spirit, and a time for renewing your enhancers with the vibrant energy of the full moon.

The following is a list of favorite full moon rituals you can do next time the moon is full!

1. Fill a pitcher or jug with water and leave it out overnight in the light of the full moon. The next day, use this water to cleanse your crystals and reinvigorate them with the energy of the full moon! Use this re-energized water to not only cleanse your crystals, but to wash your face and feel renewed from this pure energy blast, or wash counters, floors—anything you feel could benefit from the magical full moon!

2. You recently cleansed or smudged your crystals? Take it one step further and place your crystals on the windowsill for the evening, or put them in a crystal bowl and leave them outside under the light so that they can capture the moon's energy directly!

3. Use the full moon for prosperity! It is said that during a full moon you should leave your wallet and checkbook open for them to receive the moon's full energy. It may not bring you millions, but it may help to ensure that you have enough for the month to pay the bills!

4. Do you enjoy the traditional symbolic Feng Shui? Then, I'm sure you've heard about the Feng Shui money frog or toad. Legend has it that this mythical creature appeared every full moon by or near homes that would receive abundance—whether it be wealth or good news! If you have him, place him in the light of the moon, and in the morning, return him to your wealth area or place him inside by your front door, looking in!

5. Looking for love? In a red ceramic or glass bowl, arrange stones or glass beads in the bowl (purple, red, and pink work well). Next, stand up three red or pink candles in the bowl. Light the candles on the night of the full moon and focus on the light burning against the moon. Ensure your intention is that this light will bring you love—new love—or deeper love!

6. Your own power image! You've read many times that an image of a moon brings renewed energy, focus, and concentration. What better image than one you take with your own camera—a full moon you've seen with your own eyes! Print it and place it on your desk or your child's desk for increased focus!

7. The high potency of the full moon encourages fertility, passion, and abundance. Write your wishes for them with a silver pen and then burn them in a candle flame under this full moon!

8. Moon meditation is extremely powerful as the full moon is a time to draw down the energy of the moon and connect to it. Call us for a guided moon meditation!

9. Finally, don't forget the most important point—Stand in the moonlight and truly enjoy the moment for all its beauty.

THE LUNA SECRETS OF THE MOON

A person's horoscope is heavily influenced by the moon. The placement of the moon and the link between the sun and the moon is one of the major influences. It describes your emotional feelings and your ability to nurture, and it affects your mood and your reaction to the moods of others.

However, there is a lunar secret that is very important to take into consideration when your horoscope is being analyzed. When you look at the moon to determine the mood of a person, you have to look for the cycle the moon was in at the time of birth of the person.

New moon, crescent, first quarter, gibbous, full, disseminating, last quarter, and balsamic moon are called "the Lunar Cycle" and they can help you understand the moods of a person. These lunar cycles represent subtle feminine energy and power in your chart.

By finding the placement of the moon in your chart, you will be able to clarify why a person may have certain moods and often get into similar situations without realizing why.

For instance, if your moon were in the new moon phase, which lasts about three and a half days, then your mood would generally be one of emergence.

The new moon is for planting and creating. So, the kind of mood for this person would be one of hopefulness for the future, generally perceiving the world as a place of possibilities and living a life of joy.

The next lunar cycle is the crescent moon. The person with the moon in this position has a strong urge to overcome pressure and inertia of the karmic past, and by working through these issues they often discover personal limits and their special purpose. This position is from three and a half to seven days after the new moon.

During the first quarter, the half of the moon lights up. During this phase you are able to take action in implementing your new moon intention, it is time to make decisions and overcome any resistance you may face.

The gibbous moon phase is ten and a half to fourteen days after new moon, and with this position, you have an intense energy of overcoming past and present issues. You believe that whatever decisions have been made must now be lived with. This is a time of testing and adjustment; flexibility and perseverance are qualities that need to be nurtured.

Full moon is when it is opposite the sun. This position has to do with your relations of the heart, like marriage, and can cause a constant feeling of insecurity in which you may wonder if your partner is really happy with you. Learn to be happy within yourself and do not let your partner control your moods.

Next is the disseminating phase, which is three and a half to seven days after the Full Moon. This is a time where you begin to understand your inner struggles and are able to let go of them because you now understand what is underneath them.

The last quarter is seven to ten and a half days after the full moon. This position represents the harvest and meaning of understanding and whatever does not harmonize with the growing consciousness and understanding cannot be accepted.

The eighth and final phase of the entire cycle is the balsamic which occurs during the ten and a half to fourteen days after the full moon. The general mood of this cycle is release and a period when emptying is necessary before a new cycle can begin.

The balsamic moon people are old souls who have lived before and are here to complete and put into use those gifts that they have already attained, hence fulfilling a past vision.

Tips for Discernment

Discernment is an important talent for every magician. It's how we tell the difference between magic and the everyday, between truth and our imagination, and how we avoid being duped or influenced. Everyone does this inadvertently, but for a novice, intentionally honing the skill might be challenging.

Here are a few pointers, tactics, and approaches that have proven to be beneficial to me.

Make a list of everything. Record the details of what you experience, say, observe, etc., while performing a spell or interacting with a spirit. This will offer you something objective to reflect on afterward, which will be quite useful for any post-research work. You never know what information will lead to a lead.

Make a "signs" rule and stick to it. What are your thoughts on coincidences? When do you suppose a message from Nature or your gods is being sent to you? Develop a litmus test/threshold for what you perceive to be a sign; it doesn't matter what it is as long as it is applied consistently. Instead of worrying/wondering about the little details, you'll save your energy for the more essential things.

The "three-way rule" (NOT to be confused with the Wiccan Rede.) This is a popular technique for determining the above idea. An instance is when you see something for the first time, a coincidence is when you see something for the second time, and a message is when you see something for the third time. Be explicit when requesting signage. Ask for something unusual/unique enough that you wouldn't expect it to happen in the first place, but not so uncommon that it has no possibility of happening. A helpful way is to combine color with an object (for example, show me a purple feather). That way, you'll be able to predict what your sign will be.

The gut test. It is a method of determining whether or not an experience is real. When I'm conversing with a ghost, and something doesn't seem right, I'll stop and say to myself, "This isn't real. I'm fabricating this dialogue." Pay attention to how your stomach reacts. Is it immediately in agreement? Does it seem wrong to say that, as if the dialogue really is true and not fabricated? Is it true that the discourse was valid up to a point? Pay attention to your gut instincts and act appropriately.

The mimic test. This is a method of determining whether or not you are hearing the voice of a spirit or the voice of your own mind. If you're dealing with spirits and "hearing" a voice in your brain, try recreating it with your own inner voice. Is it possible to acquire the same voice? Is the loudness the same? If you can mimic it, you can probably dismiss it as a figment of your mind.

Practice. Practice. Practice. Make a habit of sensing the energy of your plants. Experiment with sensing your own energy. Give a detailed description of it. Sensing the energy of almost any ritual item is a good practice. Practice speaking with a spirit you believe in, such as a guide or your ancestors. Discrimination, like a muscle, becomes stronger with use and withers when neglected. To stay sharp for the big stuff, practice on little things. Don't be too hard on yourself. It's naturally humiliating to acknowledge we were mistaken about anything. And that's just a part of life that we will need to learn to accept if we want to sharpen our discrimination.

OK! Nobody's perfect! Recognizing our discernment errors makes us better practitioners since it shows that we're thinking critically about what we're doing and trying to improve. At the very worst, a practitioner who never recognizes a slip in judgment misses out on the opportunity to improve and runs a significant danger of being led down a rabbit hole and becoming progressively alienated from reality. So, be kind to yourself! Growing is a positive thing.

Part 2

The Art of Spellcrafting in Jars

"The world is full of magic things, patiently waiting for our senses to grow sharper." — W.B. Yeats

CLEANSE YOUR SPACE

Let's begin with the question, ***"What is energy?"***

You are surrounded by energy. Everything is made out of energy! You are a source of energy. Your ideas are made up of energy. Everything you perceive is made out of energy. When you comprehend how strong and mystical energy is, it's truly rather amazing.

When we talk about "negative energy" in the spiritual sense, we're talking about undesired energy or energy that doesn't make us feel good. Have you ever stepped into a location and sensed something wasn't quite right?

We all have various perspectives on life! What you see as negative energy may be perceived as good energy by someone else. Always pay attention to your gut sensations or intuition. When you sense that the energy in a location or around a certain individual is off, pay attention to the clues your body is sending to you.

Bad emotions (sadness, rage, envy, irritation, etc.) are only some of the things that may cause negative energy to stay in a location. Where there has been a death, wherever there has been any form of violence, a disagreement or a brawl, or a sickness or ailment might give you a lot of negative energy too.

It's usually a good idea to purify the area before executing a spell or ritual. This should be performed whether or not you perceive bad energy since not all bad energy is really negative...if that makes sense. Some energy is just unwelcome! For example, if you cast a love spell on Monday and then choose to do money magic on Tuesday in the same spot, the love spell's energy may still be there. This may perplex the cosmos and make manifesting your wishes more difficult.

Witchcraft is a deeply personal path to take. We all practice and develop specific standards of behavior that best suit our personalities over time, but one thing we all have in common is that when we sense that the power in a space is off, we instantly grab our sage, incense, selenite crystal, or whatever cleansing tools we prefer to use to clear the space of that unwanted energy. There are two advantages to purifying a place before a spell or ritual. It will be clear of any unwelcome energy. This will make it easier for you to explain your objectives. Plus, you'll feel more at ease knowing that any negative energy has been removed from your environment.

SMOKE CLEANSING

Smoke cleansing, also known as recaning (reekening, Anglo Saxon term), is one way you can effectively cleanse a space (and it's one of my favorite ways to cleanse). Smoke cleansing incorporates both the elements of Fire and Air to cleanse a space. The smoke will take in any negative energy and remove it instantly.

How to use plants for smoke cleansing:

Once you've established your intention—*Are you cleansing to open up your intuition and inner wisdom? Or, are you cleansing to create a sacred space to call in your big dream and manifestations?*—follow these steps:

1. Hold your plant and light the end. Let it burn slowly for a few seconds. Once you have a steady stream of smoke, allow the smoke to envelop you.

2. Walking counter-clockwise around the space, fan the smoke, focusing on the corners of the room. Corners are where stale energies accumulate.

3. Once you've covered the entire space, open a door or a window and let the old energy leave the room, flowing outward.

4. When the purification is done, you can place the plant in a bowl, allowing the ember to fade slowly.

Practice feeling into the energy of the space and notice when it changes. Some places will need more than one round of smoke cleansing.

There are so many amazing herbs that you can incorporate in your cleansing rituals to include:

SAGE is a powerful herb and a great cleansing tool to use in spells or rituals that focus on mental clarity, wisdom, and protection. It was first used by the Native Americans in smudging rituals or as an offering of prayer while connecting with the gods.

LAVENDER is a perfect cleansing tool to add energy to spells or rituals that focus on peace, joy, love, dreams, intuition, and de-stressing. If you are performing a spell or ritual with those intentions in mind, lavender would be a perfect cleansing tool to use to add energy to the spell or ritual.

ROSEMARY is great in spells and rituals that focus on love, protection, healing, or mental clarity. If you are calling upon any of these energies, rosemary would be a great herb to use as a cleansing tool to make the spell or ritual more powerful.

CEDAR is excellent in spells or rituals that focus on healing, protection, or money. If you are trying to manifest any of these three things into your life, cedar would be a great option to use to add to the intention you are putting out into the universe.

LEMONGRASS is also great in protection, passion, love, and positivity spells and rituals. If you are performing a spell or ritual with any of these intentions in mind, using lemongrass as your cleansing tool will add to the energy of the spell or ritual.

PALO SANTO

Palo santo is Spanish for *Holy Wood*. Palo santo has been used for its cleansing properties for thousands of years; it dates back to the Incan period.

Palo santo is available in different forms: wood, aromatic resin, and oil. The wood is available in sticks, chips, or powder, and it is 100% wood. This wood contains a potent aromatic resin that can be extracted and used separately. The oil can be derived from the wood or fruit.

In the case of cleansing the space, we are talking about the wood.

There is a lot of controversy regarding the use of this wood as it is being over-harvested. It is currently on the endangered list! Remember to be mindful if you use this wood. Do some research to know where the palo santo you buy comes from.

Its use is very similar to the process described above: Light a stick and let the flame burn for a couple of minutes. Then, with a spirit of gratitude, blow it out and walk through the areas you wish to cleanse, asking the smoke for its blessing and protection.

INCENSE

Incense is usually infused with one herb or resin or a mixture of different herbs and resins. We have previously talked about some amazing herbs that you can incorporate into your cleansing rituals. Here are some ideas for incorporating incense.

FRANKINCENSE is an excellent cleansing resin. It also is great for spells and rituals that aid in protection and mental clarity.

MYRRH is another amazing resin to use to cleanse a space before a spell or ritual. This resin is also great in blessing rituals and to enhance any other spells or rituals.

DRAGON'S BLOOD resin can also be incorporated into your cleansing rituals. It is also great in spells or rituals that focus on protection, banishing, and healing.

Allow a ten-second flame to burn from the tip of an incense stick. Fan out the flame and insert the stick inside an incense container, making sure the end is still glowing. Allow the incense to burn until it is completely gone.

CRYSTALS

To cleanse a space using crystal, you can place the crystals around the spell or the ritual area or do the same technique as we did with the smoke cleansing. With the crystal in your hand, start moving it in circular motions around the space. Counterclockwise to release negativity or clockwise to bring in positivity.

There are many great crystals you can incorporate in your cleansing rituals to release any negative or unwanted energy that may be polluting your space.

BLACK OBSIDIAN removes any negative energy within a space. It is a powerful protective stone and a great stone to use when you need to be and feel more grounded, as it is connected to the root chakra.

AMETHYST is an excellent cleansing crystal as it removes negativity from a space and brings in peaceful calming energy. It is connected to our third eye chakra, which also makes it a great crystal to enhance our psychic abilities. It is also very healing and protective as well.

SELENITE is a high vibrational crystal and is a powerful crystal to use to cleanse a space, tools, or even auras. It is said that selenite is one of the few crystals that does not require cleansing. It does not hold on to any negativity. I use selenite in just about all my spells and rituals.

BLUE KYANITE is similar to selenite. It is also said that this crystal does not need to be cleansed. This makes it a great cleansing crystal as it is of high vibrational energy. It connects to our throat chakra, making it an amazing crystal to use when we can't speak our truth or feel uncomfortable speaking with others.

WATER

Water is another wonderful tool to use in your cleansing rituals.

The best water to use is spring or purified water, but honestly, if all you have available to you is tap water, then that works just as well. Remember, it's the intentions that you put into the tools you use that makes the magic manifest.

To use water by itself, you can add it to a bowl, dip your fingers into the water, and sprinkle it around the space and over the tools you will be using.

To add power to your water, you can go different ways:

1. You can infuse your water with salt, which is a powerful combination, as water is very cleansing, and salt is great at removing negativity and bringing in protection to a space.
2. You can infuse your water with herbs that are also cleansing or reflect the intentions you have regarding the spell or ritual you are performing.
3. You can infuse your water with crystals that are cleansing or that reflect the intentions you have regarding the spell or ritual you are performing. You should always do your own research as to what crystals can and cannot be emerged into water.
4. You can infuse the water with the energy from either the moon, sun, or both! When using the moon, you can use any moon cycle you desire, but most witches love making moon water on a full moon, as that is when the energy is at its highest.

FOR MORE ADVANCED WITCHES

There are other two ways to clean the space, but I will briefly introduce them to you without going into details because I feel that they could be a bit overwhelming for a young witch.

Visualizing the space cleansed is another powerful way to cleanse a space before a spell or ritual is performed. Cleansing a space through visualization is a unique personal process and is different for everyone. It is difficult to do without the aid of other tools, such as smoke cleansing or through crystals, so, first master the basics!

Sounds are powerful and are a great tool to use to cleanse a space before spell work. Sounds produce waves that flow through the air and into our ear canal. There are many different ways to go about it: clapping, singing bowls, bells, using your own voice.

Set the Right Intent

"Only When You Release Your Intentions into the Fertile Depths of Your Consciousness Can They Grow and Flourish."

- Deepak Chopra -

~

Witchcraft is a practice involving the use of magic. Stop second-guessing yourself. You may attempt to remember what each stone does, what each herb is good for, and what each moon phase means, but if it doesn't stand true to you, it won't help you. As a result, make sure you interpret everything in your own unique way that makes sense to you. You may choose whether labradorite promotes inner beauty due to its hidden flashes of color, thyme encourages you to appreciate the tiny things, or the waxing moon boosts plant development as the moon becomes bigger.

Deciding what feels good to you and putting your purpose into its application will be much more helpful than regurgitating something half-heartedly because it's "proper." An intention is simply determining what you want to get out of a spell and conveying it as clearly and explicitly as possible to the cosmos, your intuition, higher power, deities, or whatever/whoever you're co-creating your magic with. Another reason to establish an intention is to avoid manifesting something you don't want by mistake. The truth is that the majority of the spell's strength will come from your purpose. To become clear on what you want, a terrific approach is to write it down. You must be specific...here's a basic yet powerful formula: Your intention is made up of your wish (as explicit as you are comfortable with) and the time period you want to manifest it in (if it makes sense for you). Fill up the blanks with a couple of examples of purpose written using the formula given. ("This summer, I'll be driving a tan Jeep Wrangler to my family reunion," for instance, is more effective than "Send me a new automobile.") It's not so much about making an intention as it is about making the correct intention. You must put your intention to the test and try out all of these procedures until you discover one that suits you. The components symbolize your aspirations, so choose items that embody what you desire and send your message out into the cosmos! You are the power, and the jar spells are a focus.

Using intent in charm and incantation spells enables you to concentrate on the result you wish to achieve. Spells are often used for protection and healing, but they may also be employed to make someone happy or lucky. An incantation may also utilize intent. An incantation uses words with purpose. For example, when someone casts a spell to make themselves feel better, they are using words to make themselves feel better. While incantations use words to convey meaning, chants utilize sounds or rhythms to convey intent. This technique may be used to draw attention or to relax when we are agitated. Mantras are used to express intent. We may use mantras to remind ourselves or others of something. They may be chanted, sung, or simply said out loud. Mantras are often employed for protection and self-confidence, but they may also be utilized for healing and uplifting us when we are depressed. Intent may be expressed via prayers. Prayer is when we convey our desires or thoughts. Using the words 'please grant me the strength to finish my project' as an example of a prayer would suggest asking for aid in reaching your aim.

One of the most important aspects of intent is that it always comes from the heart and not from your head. It is very easy for thoughts to automatically flow through our heads, and instead of focusing on what they are actually saying, we are only focusing on what they mean.

TOOLS FOR SETTING THE RIGHT INTENT

Setting a strong, clear purpose is one of the finest methods to energize your spell. My prior experiences have taught me that a witch's purpose is critical to any spell work.

Here are four great self-discovery tools!

Journaling for setting goals - Keep note of your spell outcomes for trends. Is it true that certain intents outperform others? Goal-setting is a very personal process, and it takes experience to uncover what works for you. I think the spells you cast with good intentions will become more reliable with time.

Spiritual connection - Great approach to discover more about yourself! Close your eyes and relax. Decide on your interactivity for this meditation. A greater power, deities, spirit guides, or even the cosmos. Ask this force, "What do I want?" Then pay attention. As you sit, pay attention to your thoughts. Throughout this meditation, be aware of any sounds, smells, or tastes. Maybe that's your power speaking to you. Don't worry if you get no response or merely a partial response. Rephrase the question you may ask about it.

Visualizing your goal - Visualization allows you to 'see' your intended result like a movie in your head. It's simple. Imagine (in one static scenario) how your life would be after you reach your objective. Pick a good moment that best represents life after your spell expires. Try changing the scenario in your visualization if anything doesn't seem right. Make all required modifications until you get what you want.

State your goal - Simply talk about your desires. It's often simpler to spot faults and positives in somebody else's plan than in our own. Your closest friend may have a better grasp of your desires than you. While friends and mentors may be helpful, you should always follow your instincts.

WHAT IF SETTING INTENTIONS HASN'T WORKED?

It's likely that you aren't adhering to the spiritual rules of the universe and honoring the "secret" to manifesting your wishes if you aren't following them.

What exactly is the secret? It's a wave of vibration!

When you direct your energy and light toward what is achievable rather than toward what you are afraid of or what you miss, you bring yourself into vibrational harmony with your goals and aspirations, allowing them to manifest. Consider the following scenario: Fear is a stumbling hurdle in the path of your goals being realized. Love and light are the catalysts for change! Allow yourself to be free of fear and come into your open heart. Elevate your vibration and tap into the brilliance of your Higher Self by meditating on this. Your intentions are far more potent when you are in this condition because they are emanating from a position of presence, love, and light.

HOW TO GET RID OF BLOCKS AROUND YOUR INTENTION

Blocks are unpleasant ideas, emotions, or worries that prevent you from achieving your goal. When casting spells, this is a relatively regular occurrence. Because they mainly emerge from your subconscious mind, blocks may be deceptive. As a result, you may not even be aware that you have any barriers. There are a few methods to figure out whether you have any blockages that need to be cleared before you cast your spell. One method is just to announce your desire aloud and pay attention to any bothersome sensations that arise when you do so. Were you concerned that you'd have to pay greater taxes since you'd be earning more money? Are you worried that once you start manifesting financial prosperity, your friends or family would beg you for money?

Another technique to discover blockages is to consider your present circumstances and make a list of all the positive aspects of it. For instance, if you want to attract a soulmate into your life, consider the advantages of being single. For this one, you'll need to think hard. Even if it's just a minor item, there's always something positive about your present circumstances. If you're single, you like getting together with your single buddies for a night on the town. Examine that assumption. Is it a stumbling block? Possibly. You are the only one who knows for sure. Take note of how you're feeling.

Do you worry that your friendship with your single pals may deteriorate? If that's the case, consider how you may approach the situation differently. Perhaps you persuade yourself that relationships change all the time and that change is necessary for progress. You might also remind yourself that your buddies are fantastic and that they will adore you regardless of your romantic state. You could discover that you have a huge roadblock in the way of your goal. If you find yourself thinking things like, "One advantage of being single is that I do not have to worry about becoming like my parents," you should investigate more. Working through larger chunks may be done in a similar way. Begin by posing a series of questions to yourself about this area. Consider the following scenario: What have my parents taught me about things I don't desire for myself? What was it about my parents' relationship that was so lovely? Can I embrace that each two-person relationship is absolutely unique, and that my relationship will never be identical to my parents'? Is there a way for me to view things from my parents' perspective and feel sympathy for them?

Is there anything I need to forgive my parents for?

Is there anything I need to forgive myself for?

Examine the responses to your questions to see if you can restructure your thinking to get past your stumbling block. When you can consider a barrier without experiencing any unpleasant emotion related to it, you've healed it.

Take it easy on yourself. Some of your roadblocks have been with you for years, and breaking through them may take some time. This is an advanced degree of self-analysis, and it takes a lot of confidence even to start looking at your roadblocks. As you investigate your obstacles, you may want to chat with family or friends or get help from a mental health expert. Alternatively, don't!

What's more, guess what? Whether or not you've freed all of your blockages, your magic remains potent. This is a never-ending process, and no one is ever completely "block-free." We're just human, after all. We have the ability to be both faulty and miraculous at the same time.

Pre-Magic Routine

It's critical to have a pre-magic regimen! It will prepare you for your spell by increasing your energy and giving you time to collect your components. Before doing magic, most magical traditions recommend that you...ground and center yourself, ritually cleanse and purify your area, and create a circle. You might even begin with some simple candle magic before making your spell jar.

Many of the practitioners of witchcraft perform rituals to get in touch with the powers. However, some witches use spells for protection or for revenge against their enemies. There are very specific rituals that need to be followed correctly before casting magic spells.

Spells usually have a lot of materials, and these should also be properly used in a certain way in order for the spell's effects to work properly. The ritual is not always an easy thing because it could take anywhere from a week to a year for a spell to actually work, depending on how complex it is and what you're trying to achieve with it.

First of all, you should have faith and a high concentration while preparing for a ritual. Also, do not leave the place during this period, or else the magic will fade away and will not work anymore. That is why, before performing any ritual, you should make sure that everything is set up properly and you feel ready.

The next step is to perform specific techniques like meditation and chanting in order to communicate with your "gods." The spellcaster needs to be in peace and quiet if he wants his spell to work; this prevents any distraction from destructive energies that could threaten its success.

Pre–Magic Ritual

This is a pre-magic ritual that I perform very often before my spells.

What You Need:

One white candle for peace, tranquility, and relaxation
One blue candle for focus, calm, and relaxation
One grey candle to keep negativity at bayRelaxing music
One tiny crystal: Aventurine for meditation and inner calm
One little moonstone crystal for serenity, balance, and protection
One tiny crystal: rose quartz (for serenity, relaxation, and stress relief) or quartz (for clearing bad energy, balancing, and aiding focus)
One incense (balancing), juniper berry, patchouli (comforting; stress relief), lavender (equilibrium, stress relief), vanilla (comforting), or sandalwood (all uses)
Peppermint oil (optional) for stress relief and spiritual energy

What's Next:

Conjure up a magical circle. Light the incense, switch on the music, and focus for a few seconds on your purpose while enjoying the wonderful aroma of your incense and the soothing sound of the music until you are ready to proceed.

Position the grey candle to the left, the white candle to the right, and the blue candle in the middle (but put the blue one a little bit forward so it can form a triangle).

To begin, light a grey candle and hold the crystal in your palm. Say:

"Grey, like the storm from which I seek shelter.

I'm free of any negativity in my environment.

Only pleasant emotions are allowed tonight.

Assist me in savoring my tranquilly."

Close your eyes for a moment. Observe how negativity diminishes. Nothing can invade without your consent, as you see a grey light emanating from the flame and creating a 'bubble' around you. Infuse your crystal with some of that protecting energy.

Open your eyes. The white candle should be lit. You should already be feeling more relaxed as you say:

"For a long time, pure white light has brought calm,

tranquilly, and pleasure to mankind."

My head had been tired for a time and was beginning to hurt beneath the strain.

For the time being, grant me a calm mind."

Close your eyes once again and let a flood of dazzling, white light enter your mind. Allow your mind and ideas to be cleared. Transfer some energy into your crystal if you think your mind is clear.

Open your eyes. The blue candle should then be lit.

"As calm and as blue as the sea,

It's important to keep your cool and relax.

Please infuse me with this frame of mind.

That I must maintain complete relaxation."

For the final time, close your eyes. Wrap the blue light from the candle tightly around your body and allow it to penetrate your being. Allow yourself to get carried away by the music and let your thoughts roam. Don't be shy in expressing yourself. Do it as long as you have the ability to concentrate. After that, put some energy back into your crystal.

Re-open your eyes. Then, take a drop of peppermint oil and dab it on your forehead, as well as a drop on your crystal. Say:

"For the time being, I am peaceful and comfortable."

Allow me to savor this moment for a little longer.

"As it is my desire, so be it."

Extinguish the candles (they can be reused when you clean them; the same goes for the crystal).

Reverse the circle's direction.

Allow the incense to burn down naturally.

Keep the crystal with you at all times. It saves the energy and will make it easier for you to enter this frame of mind anytime you need it.

P.A.

How to Create Jar Spells that Work

Are you ready to enhance your magic, improve your intent, and get amazing results from your bottle spells all at once?"

~

Container spells are as old as any magical religion known. These versatile spells are for tweaking almost any situation you can think of, from spicing up a relationship to banishing someone away from you forever. The spells being concealed and concentrated into a jar makes it a much more potent way to do your root-work. Having a spell contained in a jar also gives you a better chance of it working before it has a chance to escape.

Everyone has their own method of practicing magic, as well as their own personal preferences and rituals for what they like to do before they begin. Please, keep in mind that the material below is given as though your specific pre-magic ritual has already been done.

When it comes to making a witch bottle, be inventive and considerate!

1.   CHOOSE A VESSEL OR BOTTLE YOU WISH TO USE

You may use any empty bottle that can be filled and sealed as your container. Bottles or jars made of glass or pottery work well. Which, in theory, should be the same size and form as your intention. You may wish to use a tiny, corked bottle to support a spell candle or for shorter, "single-burner" spells. If you're making a witches' bottle for protection, you'll need something a bit larger to accommodate all the components, and it should be amber or another opaque color so you can't see inside. Your jar or bottle should ideally include a lid for different spell-mechanics functions, such as sealing the jar, keeping the contents together when shaking it, and so on. Sometimes you will need to bury a spell bottle or keep it in your house, so you may want to choose something that is easy to handle.

2.   GATHER THE CORRESPONDING CONTENTS GOING INSIDE

Items that match to the person or circumstance you're aiming to influence may be placed within your bottle. The contents of your bottle were picked for their recognized uses or for how the object(s) connect to a scenario or activity. The purpose and significance of the things within your bottle are referred to as "correspondence" by witches. Arrange harmonious ingredients that correlate to your aim. For example, if I were to construct a spell bottle for stability, I'd try to grab a few herbs and reagents that correlate to my purpose (coriander, sea salt, etc.), that are often yellow (the color I associate with balance), and keep it to five ingredients (the number I associate with balance). If money is your goal, you could use cinnamon as well as thyme in the witch bottle; you could use lavender, tiny bits of rose quartz, or a lock of your intended's hair if love is your aim; sage or salt water if cleansing or protection is your goal; and even knotted string as well as black pepper to bind somebody's ill will against you. You have complete control over the pairings and possibilities. You'll discover some suggestions to get started in a few pages! Before mixing everything, I like to scatter my ingredients about the container like tiny offerings.

3.   CHARGING

Place your intent and purpose within the contents of the bottle. Also known as "charging" the contents.

To begin, use sage, cedar incense, or palo santo to cleanse your materials. Fold a piece of paper with your purpose written on it. The number three means development, inspiration, direction, and manifestation; thus, I fold mine three times. Take a few seconds to think about your goals.

4.   FILL THE JAR WITH THE INGREDIENTS

This is where you begin your spell preparation!

Place the items inside the bottle that correspond to your intent and/or the person it is meant for.

First, fill the magic jar with the biggest or densest object (such as rock salt or crushed diamonds). In the center, place medium-weight or finely ground goods (like dried, mashed lavender flower), and on top, place the lightest, fluffiest materials (bird feathers, coarsely chopped dry herbs, etc.).

Make sure your magic jar's contents are fully dry. In a magic jar, fresh herbs will swiftly decay!

However, in spell craft, rules are meant to be disobeyed, and you can get incredibly creative by violating this one! For example, I employed live elements with a sea witch magic jar, and it grew into its own microcosmic ecosystem on the altar. It's awesome!

Declare your goal aloud as you add each object to your magic jar. Always remember to phrase things as though they are occurring right now. If you wish to jiggle the contents to reawaken them every now and then, leave some space at the top.

Pins or nettles, either inserted within the bottle or lodged in the stopper or cork to "fend off" anybody (or anything) from upsetting the bottle, are an essential component that is usually employed when making witch bottles (and is nearly as vital as the original bottle itself). If put within, these artifacts also work to trap your purpose. Many of the ancient witch bottles discovered so far have sharp "thorns" affixed to them to keep nosy hands at bay. Make sure to include this while making your bottle to ensure that it is not damaged or handled if it is ever discovered.

For more powerful spells, you may wish to add some more oomph to your jar by tying a corresponding ribbon around it or inscribing a sigil or planetary sign on it.

5.   CASTING THE SPELL

Now that your spell preparations are finished, you'll need to find an appropriate moment to conduct your spell and a mechanism to "activate" it—that is, the mechanic that will put your intent in action and accomplish the actual "casting." You'll want to choose something that, once again, aligns to your intention when it comes to timing: you may utilize the moon's waxing and waning tides to attract or repel something from your life, utilize sunsets and sunrises for manifestation and banishment, spell at high noon for an elemental fire effect, or spell on a clear day....do some study and trust your instincts!

When it comes to casting, there are many options. Here are a few common spell elements that you may mix and combine (but note, you can always design a better approach for your own spell!).

Sealing with a candle - An excellent approach to finish and perform your spell, with the additional benefit of permanently sealing the contents of your jar. Choose your candle's color to match your intention, inscribe it with a rune or symbol, anoint it with oil, or modify it in any manner you see fit to match your intention and the contents of the jar. To cast a spell in one go, burn the whole candle at once, or fire a little portion of the candle each night during the waxing or declining moon to attract or rid, respectively. White is often used as a universal replacement for any other color candle in candle magic, whereas black is useful for dispelling negativity.

Burying the jar - Bury your jar in the ground, whether in your yard or in a container, for spells concerning the earth, asserting a claim on your own land, magic you don't wish to undo, or jars honoring chthonic spirits.

Reversible spells - To lock the magic in, leave the jar's lid or cork undone by wax, but tightly held on, maybe with a thread or ribbon. You may open the jar, securely unenchant and dispose of the contents, and wipe out the jar with water and salt for later use if you ever need to undo the spell.

Re-castable spells - Before closing your jar or bottle, leave enough space in it and give it a good shake when you wish to recast.

6.   PLACE THE BOTTLE IN ITS RESTING PLACE

Once you've closed your magic bottle, don't open it until your goal has been achieved. Place your magic bottle in the most logical location for you. Keep it near your office if it's a magic bottle for diverting bad energy at work. If you're using your magic bottle to help you and your partner fall in love, store it on a nightstand near your bed. Once you've completed, consider the situation to be resolved.

7.   HOW TO SEAL A SPELL JAR

Sealing magic jars serves as a symbol as much as a practical function. On the one hand, it may act as a kind of lock, ensuring that the spell remains in place. It may also be used as an urgent spell-breaking tool by attaching a spell to the seal, which will cause the spell to stop when the lid is broken. On the other hand, sealing a magic jar keeps it from being accessed and assures that its ingredients haven't been tampered with by anybody else in the house. Closeted witches and witches having roommates may find it useful in ensuring their safety. Let's look at several ways to keep your magic jar sealed!

Wax Sealing - Wax sealing is the most frequent technique of jar sealing, which involves melting a candle and lump of wax and pouring it over the cork or lid of the jar. Many people believe that wax sealing is the most significant (not to mention attractive) method to seal a magic jar: It assures the jar hasn't been disturbed, looks lovely if done correctly, and provides a simple method to "break" the spell by linking it to seal (though many strong magic jars will still need to be cleaned thoroughly to be truly undone!). Nevertheless, there are a few factors to consider in this situation. To begin, you'll need a LOT of wax to cover even a tiny jar artistically and fully, and it may be tricky to deal with. It may or may not trickle precisely like you would like it to, and you must work quickly.

Furthermore, the bigger the jar's lid, the more wax is required. It's not as simple as it seems. Second, before selecting wax sealing, examine both your surroundings and the bottles. Even if you use a car protection jar sparingly in the winter, if you often use the heater or live someplace that gets really hot in the summer, the wax will get on everything in your center console or glove box, regardless of how little you use it. Wax coating should be acceptable if you live someplace hot but you know the magic jar won't be disturbed or handled much, and if you keep it in a cool, dry spot; but if your AC isn't working or if you leave spell jars out in the sun, it may be preferable to use another sealing technique.

Inner Wax method - If you want to use candle wax but don't want to use it for sealing, you might wax the inside of the cork or the corners of the lid instead. Then, while the wax is still flexible, seal the jar. The wax will solidify and form an inner seal, which will only be broken if the cork or lid is opened aggressively. The inside wax will loosen with heat, but it will not spread! If you don't want the wax contacting the contents of your magic jar, practice first.

Sigil method - A symbol is an excellent option if your emphasis on closing your magic jar is more defensive or spell-driven than physical. On the inside or outside of the lid or cork, sigils may be drawn or taped. One of the benefits of sigils is that they're highly programmable and can be set to do a particular job; therefore, similar to connecting your spell to the seal, a sigil may safeguard your magic jar while also acting as a spell breaker in an emergency. Please remember, however, that coding a sigil in such a particular fashion requires knowledge and practice and will almost certainly result in a sigil that is quite sophisticated. If you're just getting started, I'd suggest using a simple sigil.

Tape method - On the other hand, if you don't care about appearances and just want to make sure the jar remains closed, you could easily tape it shut! Of course, based on the tape you pick, there are ways to make this process more attractive, but in a pinch, plain old tape can do! Simply remember to cleanse and consecrate it first. As previously stated, you may use this approach in conjunction with the Sigil Method to better affix a sigil to the lid or cork and keep the jar closed. That way, you'll be able to cover all of your bases in terms of functionality!

Flame method - If the fire aspect of wax sealing is vital to your ritual, try sealing your magic jar with fire instead! Close the jar, then pass the sides of the lid or cork into the flame with a lighter and candle to purify and bless it. Although the heat may occasionally form a physical seal, this approach is mostly symbolic. If you use this approach, please use care as always while dealing with fire! Heat has the potential to shatter glass, so do your homework ahead of time; although a little flame should be alright, it's always best to be cautious than sorry!

Canning method - To be fair, this approach is a little out of the ordinary, and it should only be used in certain situations; nonetheless, it's an intriguing enough concept (that I came up with at 4 a.m. while writing this piece) that I thought I'd share it! This sealing process may easily be used to seal spell jars by kitchen witches or other witches with canning and preservation knowledge! (Not to mention that you can impart magical purpose into homemade jams, jellies, and preserves, but that's a topic for another day.) Obviously, this isn't a good sealing technique for the average magic jar maker; but, if you're using a jam jar for your spell, it's worth considering! The most important precaution is to ensure that your magic jar components will not be disturbed or damaged by exposure to heat and moisture in advance. Certain crystals can't be exposed to heat without being damaged, while dry components may be molded or rot away if moisture enters inside the jar.

8.   DISCARDING THE JARS

It's a smart option to have some concept of how you'll get rid of the leftovers when you've finished a spell before you start. Keep the leftovers close to you if the spell is intended to bring something to you, and discard them far away if the spell is intended to get rid of anything. Aside from that, you may use whichever disposal technique seems most comfortable to you. Take into account the sort of magic jar you're working with, however...

For jar used for protection - The things may be securely withdrawn from the jar and disposed of after the spell has been performed and the effects have materialized. Except for goods I wish to retain and those that can be cleansed with water, soil, or smoke, I am not fussy and just put them in the garbage. You may even blow on them if you're in a hurry, as long as you're attentive.

If it's a long-term spell that has to be concealed, I'd advise tucking it away in a dark cabinet, like the bathroom cupboard or the rear of a closet shelf. If it was previously filled with rusty nails as well as other "shrapnel" things, I'd recommend filling this jar with urine and/or vinegar and burying this jar somewhere in your yard. On the other hand, you could always leave it on somebody's doorstep...

For a jar used as a reflection jar - The reflecting jar and its reflecting contents should be carefully cleaned and dried before being placed in a window to receive sunlight and moonlight for at least 28 days. If the witch jar is put in a window to mimic the sun or moon's light, it should not be used for more than a year and a day. ('A Year and a Day; is equal to 13 Lunar Months of 28 days each plus a day for the sun.) It's the equivalent of 365 ordinary days!) After which, this witch's jar has to be opened and emptied. Any spells, sigils, or other paper items in the jar should be burnt and buried with a circle cast and blessing offered to bring the spell to a close. The jar is now ready to be reused.

For organic-matter-containing jars - Put on rubber gloves and gently open the jar, emptying the components into a trench before burying the jar and contents to decay! Then, to terminate the jar's spell, raise the circle and cast a Blessing Spell!! If the jar is challenging to open, bury it and continue with your circle!

When Your Jar Spell Fails

No witch can guarantee that her spells will work 100 percent of the time. Here's a quick rundown of what may have caused a spell to fail, as well as some potential fixes.

Distraction - if you're not engrossed in a spell, it won't have any power.

Rosemary - according to legend, may be used to substitute anything. It provides generic pow-er, but what good is that power if you don't add something to the spell that has any real value for you? Where does all that energy go when it has nowhere to go?

Associations - although everyone else's list of correspondences for herbs, stones, and planets might be extremely beneficial, you may have an opposing personal connection.

Didn't assist the spell - spells can only do so much, and they are unlikely to succeed if you don't put up the effort. If you don't fill out applications, job spells won't function.

Too many cooks - if you cast ten love charms and no one is drawn to you, it's likely that they all worked but were incompatible with one another, canceling each other out.

Aim for the stars - there are instances when you strive to accomplish something, and your ex-pectations are unrealistically high. Either it's impossible, you're approaching it incorrectly, or you didn't achieve what you wanted.

Cancellation - a spell may seem not to work when it really works, but the consequences are hidden because something else was canceled out.

Impatient - the magic may be functioning, but you aren't seeing the benefits yet unless you set a working time restriction into it. It may take some time to complete these tasks.

Feeling out of your depth - if you don't feel ready to cast a spell, the lack of confidence and low vi-brations might either deactivate the magic or make it ineffective.

WHAT YOU SHOULD DO:

1. Take a breather, ground yourself, purify yourself, and give it time. Refocus your goals and ob-jectives.
2. Consider each element and step in a spell, and make any necessary changes.
3. Stick to the components you know work best for you; old standbys are still valid.
4. Consider what you might do to aid the spell's effectiveness.
5. Pause for a moment and assess the situation objectively. Is there another way to look at it, or can you narrow it down into chunks?
6. Start with the spells you're most familiar with and work your way up.

Part 3

White Magic in a Bottle

"The world will always need "magic". Without it, Life is nothing but cheap tricks." – Solange Nicole

"I Am Attracting Opportunities
That Align With My Dream Life.
I Attract What Serves
My Highest Good."

~

WHITE MAGIC

Magic doesn't necessarily have an official color system, but people usually will describe it as white or light if the spell doesn't harm or influence the will of another. White Magic is the safest of all spell types and is a good place to start if you're a beginner because there are no potentially negative consequences to misdirecting your intention.

Healing and protection rituals are some of the oldest spells known. Healers were integral parts of villages, and their studies in herbalism and health are what went on to become modern medicine.

These spells are an important part of any witch's arsenal and will prepare you for anything you encounter on your path. You don't have to follow each step exactly. Do what feels natural to you, so your energy may flow constantly.

QUANTITIES

You will find that most ingredients in this book are not in exact quantities. This is intentional as it's not based exactly on how much you need of each; it's more to do with how much of something you can acquire or have on hand. Quantities are also based on how much you feel as an individual will fit inside your jar. These spells are customizable and not exact. The recipes you find in this book are the ones I have used and have perfected over the years. You may find that you are moved to use something else or add a trinket of some sort, and that is perfectly ok! It will be more customized to your needs and to you as an individual. So, keep the creativity alive!

Acceptance

This is a spell is for self-acceptance when you need to remind yourself that you are perfect, just the way you are.

WHAT YOU NEED:

* Pink or red candle for love and acceptance
* White candle for understanding and communication
* Amethyst for communication, love, peace
* Azurite for acceptance
* Tiger's eye for acceptance
* Lavender for peace, stability, happiness
* Rosemary for love, acceptance
* Lemon Balm for understanding
* Sigil for acceptance/understanding - optional
* Honey to sweeten the situation

WHAT'S NEXT:

1. Cleanse the stones, crystals, and herbs if needed.
2. Light the candles and think of your intent of the spell.
3. Visualize the acceptance and love you will receive.
4. Put the ingredients into the bottle, whispering:

   "Everything I've ever needed, and everything I'll ever need, is now inside me. This strong, Divine body and spirit are loved and accepted by me."

5. If you like, you could also add in the Wunjo rune for joy, happiness, and peace.
6. Seal the bottle with the red and white candle wax.

Anti-Anxiety

This spell is an anxiety-busting charm, helping you find some much-needed grounding and easing those subconscious saboteurs. Keep it close by any time you need a boost of calming energy.

WHAT YOU NEED:

* White candle
* Pink Himalayan salt for banishing negativity and fear
* Tiger's Eye chips for inner strength and courage
* Lavender for peace and calm
* Chamomile for relaxation and soothing

WHAT'S NEXT:

1. Add each ingredient to your jar, focusing on your intentions.
2. Light the white candle.

3. Take 3 deep breaths while holding your jar.
4. Repeat the following 3 times:

"Nervous anxiety, you are dead.
May the items in this jar soothe my head.
Bring me your calming peace.
Anxiety thoughts you will now cease."

5. Seal your jar with wax from your candle and use it as a charm or talisman.

Anti-Depression

A manifestation jar to alleviate issues associated with depression, anxiety, and low self-esteem.

WHAT YOU NEED:
* Roses for self-love
* Lavender for healing
* Himalayan pink salt for emotional and personal empowerment, healing wounds, and dissolving self-doubt
* Clear quartz for purifying the aura and soul, balancing emotions
* Citrine for increasing self-esteem and focus
* Lemon verbena for self-improvement
* Spearmint for transformation
* Thyme for driving away negativity

WHAT'S NEXT:
1. Place all the contents in a jar, and keep on a window sill or porch, somewhere with lots of light.

Art Productivity

A spell jar made to help improve your art skills and productivity. It is filled with positive vibes and lots of love. It helps to stimulate creativity, boost self-confidence, and achieve success in your artistic work.

WHAT YOU NEED:
* Lavender to get rid of anxiety
* Grass to aid in spiritual visions
* Marigold to strengthen sight
* Carnelian to stimulate creativity
* Cinnamon for personal power and success in work

WHAT'S NEXT
1. Add everything to a bottle and keep it nearby while working.

Astral Projection

This potent white magic bottle spell will help your soul leave your body during your astral projection, aka the *Out of Body Experience*.

WHAT YOU NEED:

*   Sea salt for protection, connected to water
*   Black salt for protection against negativity
*   Myrrh incense ash for divination, energy amplifier
*   Dragon's blood incense ash for protection, banishing
*   Cracked black pepper for banishing, protection
*   Lavender for dreams, meditation, peace of mind
*   Chamomile for peace, anxiety reliever
*   Red rose petals for trust, divination
*   Lapis lazuli for intuition, psychic ability
*   Citrine for mental focus, clarity, confidence
*   Amethyst for intuition, psychic ability, protection, courage
*   Clear quartz for amplifier, mental clarity, focus
*   Fluorite for mental focus and clarity, smooth communication, and calming the mind
*   Sealed with black, purple, and blue wax

WHAT'S NEXT:

1. Fill the bottle, remembering the layering technique mentioned earlier where you will put the bigger and heavier items at the bottom and the lighter items at the top. The crystals in this bottle are a full layer, and the lapis is bigger stones; please adjust to the size of your bottle and supplies available.
2. I keep the bottle by the side of my bed, and I charge it with every full moon.

Astral Projection II

This second version is much simpler than the previous one - especially useful if you are starting out and don't have access to many herbs or have to keep your practice discreet!

WHAT YOU NEED:

*   White candle for purity and protection
*   Anise seed for enhanced psychic ability, warding off low vibrations in dreams, protection, happiness, cleansing
*   Bay leaf for good fortune, protection, success, strength, psychic ability
*   Black pepper for banishing and protection
*   Protection sigil(s) of your choice

WHAT'S NEXT:

1. Cleanse and charge.
2. Light the candle.

3. Cast a circle through visualization.
4. Layer the black pepper, anise, and bay leaf into the bottle.
5. Seal with white candle wax.
6. Draw and burn protection sigils to activate.

Attract Affection and Romance

You can use this little magic jar to bring willing romantic partners to you or encourage new friends or better family relations. It will work best if you carefully think about your purpose before casting the spell and use care in picking your ingredients.

WHAT YOU NEED:

* Herbs and ingredients for your purpose (for romance: Chocolate or cocoa, roses, apples, carnations, aster, jasmine) (for friendship: Buttercups, daisies, lilacs, vanilla, oranges, tea)
* Key items you associate with your purpose
* Correspondence for what you want to happen (for example, a coaster from a club you'd like to go to with new friends, a coffee so you go out on coffee dates, etc.)

WHAT'S NEXT:

1. Cleanse your bottle and empower it with your purpose, holding the jar in your hands and envisioning your intent, or writing your purpose in a couplet.
2. Select the herbs and items that feel right and are akin to your purpose.
3. Gather the ingredients together. Layer them in the jar; as you add them, you can say either verbally or in your head what you're adding to the jar.
4. Once you're happy with the jar, go ahead and close it.

Attract Happy Love

I made this jar years ago when I felt hopeless and lonely, and I honestly thought that I would never find anyone for me. Five years later...I am happily engaged!

WHAT YOU NEED:

* Lavender, for Achillean love
* Thyme to dispel hopelessness
* Sugar to attract what you desire
* Lemon balm leaves and rose petals to attract a love
* Rosemary needles for a healthy and long-lasting love
* Rose quartz or clear quartz (optional)

WHAT'S NEXT:

1. Layer the ingredients following this order: sugar on the bottom, then lemon balm, rose petals, thyme, rosemary needles, and finally lavender.
2. Focus on your heartbeats as you hold the jar and visualize a soft pink light around it, slowly lifting out into the universe for someone to find.
3. Carry it with you in day-to-day life.

Banish Fatigue

I whipped up a jar spell to banish fatigue from my life and welcome energy and healing!

WHAT YOU NEED:

* Sea salt
* Sage incense to cleanse your jar
* Coffee to provide peace of mind and grounding, and overcome internal blockages
* Sugar for joy, and sweet thoughts
* Dried dandelion flower for happiness, perseverance, and strength
* Wings of a bumblebee to make hard work easier
* Dried orange peel for love, luck, and divination
* Leaf of an African violet for healing, spirituality, and protection
* Anise seed to find happiness and stimulate psychic ability
* Basil flowers to dispel confusion, fears, and weakness
* Oregano for joy, vitality, and strength
* Rosemary for completing tasks, and improving memory
* Cloves for banishing hostile forces, and gaining what is sought
* Ginger to grow personal confidence, prosperity, and success
* Jasmine for charging, and magical energy
* Mustard seeds for courage, endurance, and faith
* Amethyst point for healing and purifying
* Yellow wax to seal
* Orange or yellow string

WHAT'S NEXT:

1. Cleanse your jar using sage incense, and layer the ingredients in your jar one at a time, with dandelion, basil, and bee wings on top.
2. Tie the amethyst around the jar using the orange/yellow string; seal it with the yellow wax.
3. Kiss the jar on the lid and thank the correspondences for the help they will bring you.
4. Place the jar nearby, and kiss it every time you need a boost of energy.

Banishment

Banishment is often the last resort, but sometimes it is necessary. Its purpose is to eliminate forces that might interfere with a magical operation, and it is usually performed at the beginning of a significant event or ceremony. But it can be performed for its own sake as well. Here is a banishing I use to calm and balance my mind, creating a sense of cleanliness within myself and the environment. Feel free to adjust to your practice.

WHAT YOU NEED:

* Shredded soap - better if grated. You can also shave it with a knife
* Moon water
* Sage

* Gem elixir (I used a mix of amethyst, clear quartz to clear away negativity, rose quartz for love and harmony, and hematite to be rid of negative energy)
* One spray bottle
* Black candle

WHAT'S NEXT:

1. In a bowl, mix the moon water, your gem elixir, and the soap. To bless the soap and gift it with spiritually cleansing properties, use this chant:

> *"Soap you clean and clear away*
> *dirt, debris, and my dismay.*
> *I bless you so you will send away*
> *everything that I do not approve."*

2. Pour this mixture into the spray bottle and add the sage.

3. Spray around yourself and your house.

4. Burn a black candle to remove the remaining negative energy.

BE NICE CHARM

Do you have an interview coming up? Or do you have a meeting with your boss and want to make a good impression? This spell will assist in creating a positive effect on whoever you wear the charm around. Perform this spell on a Sunday or during a new moon.

WHAT YOU NEED:

* Mortar and pestle or grinder
* Dried rose petals
* Dried lavender
* Dried lemon balm
* Orange zest
* Small glass jar
* Funnel
* A piece of jewelry, like a ring or necklace

WHAT'S NEXT:

1. Cleanse your altar.
2. Use a mortar and pestle to lightly grind the rose petals, lavender, lemon balm, and orange zest.
3. Focus on raising your energy and setting your intentions.
4. Pour the mixture into a small glass jar with a funnel and attach the bottle to the piece of jewelry.
5. Wear it whenever you feel the need for a bit of extra positivity.

BREAKING FREE FROM THE SHACKLES

This spell is about changing the attitudes and bad habits that keep you shackled to your limitations. As always, feel free to adjust the ingredients upon your needs.

WHAT YOU NEED:

* Magnesite for calming the mind
* Chili powder for motivation to take bigger risks to gain bigger rewards

* Cinnamon to fall in love with your life and want better for yourself
* Basil for a boost of luck and financial gain
* Salt to cleanse yourself of self-doubt
* Pen and paper
* Red ribbon for self-love
* White, red, and blue candle for purity of mind, passion for life, mental tranquility

WHAT'S NEXT:

1. Write everything you want in life. Fold the paper and place it in the bottle with the magnesite and herbs, certain that you will burn through your previous self-hating/questioning expectations and ideas of what everyone else wants so you can have a vice hold on what you desire.
2. Put on the lid or cork, tie and knot the ribbon around the jar, then seal it using white wax initially, then red, and finally blue.
3. Put it beside your bed for willpower, knowing that every time you lay down at night, you'll be reminded that tomorrow is another opportunity to go closer to achieving your goals and dreams.

CALMING

I made this spell jar for a dear friend of mine, who has been feeling very anxious and worried lately. After a couple of days, the negative energy was gone, and she felt more relaxed!

WHAT YOU NEED:

* A purple candle
* Small amethysts for their anti-anxiety properties
* Calming herbs (I use rose)
* Pink and black salt
* Eggshells
* Lavender incense
* Sea salt to promote cleansing
* Lavender to promote cleansing of the mind and body
* Chamomile for calming and inner peace
* Sage to get rid of negative energy

WHAT'S NEXT:

1. Use your lavender incense to cleanse the magic bottle. Fill the jar halfway with pink and black salt, as well as the eggshells, for safety. It's ideal to use 3 pinches of each. Add 3 pinches of each dried herb.
2. Remember to keep your attention on the goal. Add a few amethysts to the jar that are tiny enough to fit.
3. Seal the jar with the purple (preferably violet) candle wax.

ℬLESSING

Here are the ingredients I add to my blessing bottles. This acts as a starter. You can use some, none, or all of these, plus your additions. They all will play well with other components.

~

WHAT YOU NEED:

A bay leaf for luck and prosperity
Rosemary for protection
St. John's Wort for mental and emotional stability
Lavender for peace and restorative sleep
Calendula for prosperity and luck
Snake skin for gentle rebirth and rites of passage
Red stones for passion and creativity
Blue stones for peace, truth, and healthy communication
Yellow stones for joy and happiness
Orange stones for health
Green stones for prosperity and healing
Pink stones for love and self-appreciation
White stones for spiritual growth
Black stones for protection from negativity
Oils to promote your goals (I use our 5 blessings oil, showers of gold and road opener oils)
Charms/Amulets (I use a 4-leaf clover for luck, a heart for love, a key to open closed doors, and a money bag for prosperity)
A sliver of selenite to tie it all together

~

WHAT'S NEXT:

Fill all the ingredients in a bottle and say the following out loud:

"May the Goddess,
The eternal source of all creation;
And the lady of the Moon;
Horned hunter of the Sun;
May the powers of the spirits,
Rulers of the elemental realms;
May the powers of the stars and the earth,
Bless this time, this place, and I who am with you."

You can place this little jar on your altar, or in a family room or near the entrance to your home.

CLEARER DREAMS

This jar started as a sweet dreams spell, and turned into something even more important: it makes dreams clearer and easier to interpret so you can figure out what is up with your life!

WHAT YOU NEED:

* One bud of lavender for sleep and clarity
* Peppermint for happiness, and sweet dreams
* Rosehip to protect against nightmares
* Sugar to sweeten dreams
* Rosewater to sweeten dreams
* Amethyst to prevent nightmares and balance emotions
* A yellow thread as, in dreams, it represents warmth, wisdom, happiness, hope, and energy
* Yellow candle wax

WHAT'S NEXT:

1. With the yellow thread, tie the Amethyst to the jar.
2. Layer the ingredients with lavender on top.
3. Light the candle and seal the jar with the wax.
4. Charge the jar next to the burning candle.
5. Keep it near the head of your bed as you sleep.Enjoy some clearer dreams!

COMMUNICATION

For when you can't quite get your words to come out right, or there seems to be a significant miscommunication in your life.

WHAT YOU NEED:

* Vanilla incense ash (optional) for warmth and peace
* Salt for cleansing, clarifying
* Oregano to promote tranquility
* Clove to prevent malicious words
* Dill to encourage kindness, wards off ill intent
* Mint for healing and renewal
* Caraway for memory and honesty
* Citrine or lapis lazuli and blue wax

WHAT'S NEXT:

1. Clean your jar with the vanilla incense.
2. Place all the ingredients in the jar.
3. Charge with citrine or lapis lazuli.
4. Seal with blue wax!

CONFIDENCE AND SUCCESS

This is a general good fortune spell designed to attract wealth and success. The results can be interesting because they don't always manifest wealth in the way you might think, but it always brings some kind of windfall to me. Performe this spell during a full moon, preferably done on a Tuesday.

WHAT YOU NEED:

* Orange candle for encouragement, creativity, stimulation, and attraction
* Sage for protection, wisdom
* Ginger for success, boosts spells, power, protection
* Rosemary for protection, wisdom, health
* Mint for prosperity, love, joy, success
* Cinnamon for heightened energy, success, protection, confidence
* Bay for heightened success, wisdom, protection, peace, happiness
* Thyme for power, love, courage
* Salt for protection, cleansing
* Egg shells for protection
* Sharpie

WHAT'S NEXT:

1. Make a sigil with the intention you desire: Mine was centered on creating a good initial impression and being confident.
2. Write it on bay leaf with the Sharpie and place it inside the magic jar.
3. Combine all of the remaining ingredients.
4. Concentrate your energy and purpose into the bottle while being positive.
5. Close the magic jar and lock it with orange wax.
6. Keep spell jar with you whenever you need it.

COURAGE

This spell will help you push through the hard times! It provides comfort and courage in the face of an adversarial event or troubling times. Perform during a waxing moon if possible, preferably on a Tuesday.

WHAT YOU NEED:

* Clove powder for purification, banishing negative forces
* Sage herb for wisdom and emotional strength
* Peridot shards for healing and protection
* Tiger's eye shards for courage, truth, and strength
* Basil herb to bring happiness and steady the mind
* Crushed rose petals for confidence and self-love
* Thyme herb for courage and strength
* Rosemary herb for cleansing, remembrance, and healing

* Sea salt for protection, purification, and healing
* A small lapis lazuli bead to bring inner power, hope, and the strength to overcome depression, grief, and trauma

WHAT'S NEXT:

1. Set your intention, layer ingredients into the bottle, and charge.
2. Repeat the spell every day for nine consecutive days. You will start to feel a little braver within a few days.

CREATIVE WRITING

WHAT YOU NEED:

* Green Aventurine chips
* Red Agate chips
* Small conch shells
* Rose water or oil
* Moon water

WHAT'S NEXT:

1. Before commencing the magic, mix your rose oil and moon water, or add a small amount at the end. Combine the items in the bottle once you're ready.
2. Say the following when putting the ingredients in the bottle:

"Aventurine for green concepts
Adventures were done, and new areas were discovered.
Agate is a stone of inventiveness.
For fantasies and ideas
Words move via little conches.
They know where to move from the thoughts to the paper.
Rosewater sweet
Stick these three
And bring my creativity."

CREATIVITY

A simple bottle spell to promote innovative thinking and creativity. Perfect for writers, artists, designers, music artists, and more!

WHAT YOU NEED:

* Fern for mental clarity
* Basil for prosperity, wealth, creativity
* Rosemary for mental clarity, memory, creativity
* Clover for luck, success
* Pine needles for perseverance, prosperity, strength
* Wild sunflower petals for optimism, creativity
* White or orange candle or thread for sealing
* Pen and a bay leaf
* Incense (I used myrrh because it's what I had, and the scent makes me feel grounded)

WHAT'S NEXT:

1. Cleanse yourself, your ingredients, and your space. Center and ground your energy.
2. Using a pen, write your sigil onto the bay leaf. Then, charge it.
3. Empower each of your ingredients with the energies you want them to release - Burn each plant component while saying its purpose and visualizing your goal. Add the ashes and unburnt parts to your jar.
4. Seal your container while visualizing your intent.
5. Finalize your spell in your desired way and thank the energies of the herbs you used.

ᴅYSPHORIA HEALING

I specifically came up with this spell with dysphoria in mind, but it can work for anyone who needs to improve their self-perception! Remember that your intent is key.

WHAT YOU NEED:

* Sea salt for protection from bigotry
* Cloves for keeping negative energy at bay
* Lavender for tranquility, and inner peace
* Rosemary to banish dysphoria and insecurity
* Sage for wisdom, and self-growth
* Rose petals for self-love, and trust
* Tiger's eye shards for willpower, and self-confidence)
* White candle wax for protection, and guidance

WHAT'S NEXT:

1. Layer the ingredients in the jar (the order is irrelevant) while focusing on your intent, and seal it.
2. You can store it in a bag with a piece of tumbled rose quartz for extra self-love.

EMOTIONAL HEALING

This jar promotes emotional healing after a great upheaval and stresses of the heart.

WHAT YOU NEED:

* Peppermint for cleansing
* Roses to help you heal from trauma
* Blue lace agate for emotional healing
* Rock salt for cleansing
* Ivy to guard off negativity
* Rosemary oil to protect, cleanse, and purify vibrations
* Black tourmaline chips to banish negativity
* Jade crystal to promote harmony and good luck – optional

WHAT'S NEXT:

1. Add everything to a bottle and keep it in the room.

Empath Protection

Being an empath is such a curse and a blessing! I tend to go through more problems taking in negative energy from others. I often feel that I need some extra protection.

WHAT YOU NEED:

* Chamomile infused olive oil for peace and security
* Taglock of yourself (hair, blood, nail clippings)
* Back salt for purification
* Black pepper for protection
* Basil to dispel weakness
* Cinnamon for strength
* Sage to purify
* Clove to banish negative forces
* Coffee to dispel negative thoughts
* Dandelion leaf for healing and defeating negativity
* Bay for healing, strengthening psychic abilities
* A black or purple candle.

WHAT'S NEXT:

1. Add the ingredients in the jar, and while doing so, you chant:

   "I protect myself,
   As this gift can harm,
   Shall I be balanced,
   Give power to this charm."

2. Seal it with wax. Visualize and meditate.

Endless Desire

This beginner-friendly jar helps to remove obstacle from a love relationship and strengthen the bond.

WHAT YOU NEED:

* 2 red roses
* Paper and pen

WHAT'S NEXT:

1. Fill a glass bottle halfway with two red flowers. Type the complete names of the couple's two members on a bit of paper and place it inside the bottle. Once, state the following spell aloud:

   "Pact and conspire,
   crystal and flowers
   with endless desire burn in his heart."

ENERGETIC PROTECTION

This blend made of crystals and herbs and sealed with white will help you protect your aura and bring in the energies of manifestation.

WHAT YOU NEED:
* Black salt to absorb and drive out negative energy
* Rosemary to ward off negative energy and raise vibrations
* Blue vervain to clear energy
* Cedar to drive out negative energies and welcome positive ones
* Juniper berries to keep unkind energies away and to protect from theft and accidents
* White wax

WHAT'S NEXT:
1. Fill all the ingredients in the jar, focus on feeling safe and protected, and say the following:

   "My energy is precious and bright to me.
   I am deserving of protection from darkness and negativity.
   This enthusiasm will always lead me in the right direction."

2. Seal with white wax.

ENERGY AND MOTIVATION

This spell is designed to reduce fatigue and increase productivity, positive energy, and motivation. Carry it around with you when feeling unmotivated and tired, or put it near your workplace. It is also great to do morning meditations with.

WHAT YOU NEED:
* Coffee for grounding, energy, and happiness
* Cinnamon for success and motivation
* Lavender for peace and calmness
* Rosemary for intellect and memory
* Sunflower seeds for personal power and goal setting
* Orange peel for luck and success
* Bay leaf to strengthen the will
* Jasmine for creativity
* Almond for productivity
* Basil for luck and energy
* Agate chips for stability, clarity, and concentration
* Tiger's eye chips for willpower and confidence, luck
* Sigil (I used "*I have all the motivation I need to complete any task*")

WHAT'S NEXT:
1. Use dragon's blood to cleanse the jar and strengthen the spell before assembling.

Everyday Bottle Spell

A simple day-to-day supportive bottle spell.

WHAT YOU NEED:

* Himalayan rock salt for grounding
* Pink wax for self-love
* Pink rose petals for sweetness and love
* Rosemary for mental clarity
* Cinnamon for protection
* Dried lavender flowers for peace

WHAT'S NEXT:

1. Add each ingredient while you say aloud its purpose.
2. After reflecting a bit on how you've been feeling lately, write down your intentions focusing on the bottle. Put the cork in and dip it in the wax.

Fertility

This spell bottle brings fertility to an infertile couple/person. Place it anywhere that feels comfortable to you and focus on the intent you wish to receive daily.

WHAT YOU NEED:

* Eggshells for fertility
* Lavender for divine feminine
* Pink salt for love and positive energy
* Rose quartz for love
* Jasmine for pure love, growth, and youth
* Amethyst for protection
* Pink candle for birth and blessing
* Amaranth incense for healing

WHAT'S NEXT:

1. Clean the jar with the incense's smoke, add the ingredients, and seal the jar with the pink wax.

Focus

This jar is for focus, be it at work, in school, or in your daily life.

WHAT YOU NEED:

* Cinnamon powder for concentration
* Basil herb to dispel confusion and mental fatigue
* Rosemary herb for mental power
* Amethyst shards for balance, healing, and focus

* Tiger's eye shards for stability and strength
* Carnelian shards for self-esteem and focus

WHAT'S NEXT:

1. Place the ingredients in the jar while focusing on your intent.

FORGET AND MOVE ON

Memories sometimes can drag you down. This spell will help you forget your past troubles, come to terms with them and move on to better parts of your life.

WHAT YOU NEED:

* Cinnamon for self-empowerment
* Black or sea salt for purification and cleansing
* Turquoise shards for healing
* Quartz shards for moving on and purification
* Lavender sprigs for calming
* Opal shards for calming and forgetting
* Amethyst shards for healing

WHAT'S NEXT:

1. Place the ingredients in the jar while focusing on your intent.

FORGIVENESS

I genuinely love this spell for its special and unique symbolism: the onion makes you cry and weep, which symbolizes what you would do when asking someone for forgiveness.

WHAT YOU NEED:

* One small white or red onion
* A photograph of the person from whom you want to ask for forgiveness
* A red ribbon

WHAT'S NEXT:

1. Split the onion in half and place both halves into the jar.
2. Fold the photo in half with the image facing inward.
3. Place the folded photo between the onion halves forming a sort of sandwich.
4. Tie the ribbon around the lid with a double knot.
5. Close your eyes, visualize what you want to happen, and make your request.
6. Place the jar on a windowsill to charge with the moonlight—even if the moon isn't visible—for the entire night.
7. After 24 hours, bury the jar in your garden/yard, or you can take it to a local park, beach, or forest. It doesn't need to be buried deep.
8. You will notice the first signs of forgiveness within a few days.

FRIENDSHIP

This jar radiates harmony and a positive attitude between you and your friend!

WHAT YOU NEED:
* Allspice to stimulate friendly conversation and interaction
* Carnation to improve and deepen the friendship
* Cinnamon for luck, prosperity, and strength
* Lavender for protection and love
* Oregano for energy and joy
* Thyme to build loyalty
* Mint to promote energy and communication
* Rosemary for protection and healing
* Yellow and pink glitter
* Yellow candle and string

WHAT'S NEXT:
1. In a small bowl, mix the herbs and glitter.
2. Add the herbs and glitter to the jar.
3. Wrap the yellow string around the jar - Feel free to put a sigil on the lid before sealing.
4. Seal it with candle wax - Bless as you seal and speak out your intentions. For example, I asked to bless a friend with good luck and prosperity and to strengthen our bond.

GENERAL WELLBEING

I've been feeling a little out of sorts lately, so I thought I would create a revitalizing spell recipe!

WHAT YOU NEED:
* Lavender for healing, calming, protection
* Rosemary for healing, health, protection
* Dried Lemon for rejuvenation
* Jasmine for a mind free of worries

WHAT'S NEXT:
1. Write out your needs/wants/desires on a piece of paper and place it under or near your spell bottle. You may burn a candle while working your spell. Just remember, your intent is everything.

GLAMOUR SPELL

This little jar is intended to increase your beauty and attractiveness for a special event or party.

WHAT YOU NEED:
* Rose petals for love, and beauty
* Orange peel for luck, beauty, attraction, and love

* Vanilla for love, passion, lust, and likeability
* Lemongrass for attraction, and lust
* Ginger for confidence, sensuality, and catalytic properties
* Jasmine tea for love, beauty, and likeability
* Cardamom for lust
* Cinnamon for love, luck, success, and catalytic properties
* Apple seeds for transformation, and love
* Sugar for likeability, sexuality, lust, and love
* Rose quartz chips for love, and beauty,
* Jasper chips for luck, and beauty
* Tiger's eye chips for luck, and confidence
* A sigil matching intention (mine represents *"Everyone finds me gorgeous"*)

WHAT'S NEXT:

1. Light a candle matching your focus, energy, and intention if you wish.
2. Combine the ingredients in a jar, and while holding it, recite the following incantation:

"May these flowers, spices, and peel Grant me charm, beauty, and appeal.
Lovely and ravishing shall I be with these stones, seeds, and tea.
Lovely and ravishing shall I be.
I will emanate a radiant light that will be seen all day and night.
With stunning looks and alluring dance, all those around me I shall entrance."

3. Seal with wax, charge the jar with moonlight the night before the event, and carry it with you when you go. Alternately, you could enchant a piece of jewelry or any other objects you will have with you by putting them in the container with the ingredients and leaving them to charge.

GOOD CLARITY AND LUCK

Clarity is about removing the mental junk we accumulate during the day and seeing our truths to the core. This spell helps to sweep away unwanted thoughts, and it is best performed on Wednesday.

WHAT YOU NEED:

* Green candle
* Peppermint oil
* Bergamot oil
* Basil
* Catnip
* Lavender
* Bay leaf
* Cloves
* Chamomile
* Rosemary
* Cinnamon
* Marigold
* Tiger's eye
* Aventurine
* Frankincense

WHAT'S NEXT:

1. Perform the pre-spell routine, which includes lighting frankincense, cleansing green candle using incense smoke, and anointing the candle using bergamot oil.
2. Before placing each component in the jar, pass it through incense smoke. Say out loud what the item will be used for as you put it in the container.

3. Before placing the bay leaves in a jar, write a good luck symbol, a sigil for attention, and a sigil for excellent memory on each leaf (one per leaf). If the leaves need to be folded, fold them towards you, then flip them to the right and fold them back towards you. You wish to draw good fortune and prosperity to yourself.

4. Fill the container with seven drops of peppermint oil.

5. While keeping your hands over the magic jar, recite this affirmation while channeling your energy and intentions:

"I am concentrated, I am smart.
Look into my heart; I am not a liar.
Please provide me luck and clarity.
So, I'm confident that I'll pass, and I'm certain that I'll succeed.
Because of my incredible memory, I want my concentration and strength to always be on my side.
My work will not be a frenzied mind.
Earth, fire, wind, and the sea are the four elements that make up the universe.
As I have spoken, so must it be!"

6. To charge the spell, seal the container with candle wax and lay it among the crystals. You're prepared to take on that test after the candle has burned all the way down!

GROUNDING AND SECURITY

This little jar helps to quell emotional turmoil and help provide a sense of safety. I love holding it tight in my hands when I feel overwhelmed. Alternatively, you could also keep it on your nightstand.

WHAT YOU NEED:
*   Nutmeg for grounding and comforting energy
*   Oregano brings comfort and healing
*   Chamomile for calming, and comforting
*   Thyme has a similar use as the oregano with more of the healing and calming properties that I find similar to chamomile, and I love how these two herbs work together
*   Tree bark to lock in a sense of security and add a personal touch. It is also really great for grounding

WHAT'S NEXT:
1. Cleanse and empower your jar.
2. Gather the ingredients together and layer them in the jar.
3. Once you're happy with the jar, go ahead and close it.

Happiness

Do you pick up good vibrations? This little bottle of happiness has been created to help you add more positive vibes to your day.

WHAT YOU NEED:

* Linden leaf for joy, luck, and happiness
* Basil for luck, happiness, and peace
* Jasmine for happiness and sweet dreams
* Marigold for peace and luck
* Sage for purification
* Vervain for protection and purity
* Himalayan Sea Salt for banishing negativity

WHAT'S NEXT:

1. Put on some happy songs with high vibration.
2. Layer the ingredients.
3. You can use the bottle as a charm or seal it with yellow and white wax on top for joy, purification, and happiness of course.

Healing for Childhood Trauma

This ritual might be best performed on a Sunday—the day of the sun. I would also suggest you do a full cleanse with smoke or shower before performing this bottle spell and pouring yourself into the chant, letting the words vibrate through you!

WHAT YOU NEED:

* Salt (either black or pink Himalayan salt)
* Small healing crystals (I use tangerine quartz and angel aura quartz, but it's up to you)
* Small items from your childhood
* A drop of your blood - optional
* Scent or herbs that remind you of your childhood
* Raw honey
* A green string as green is known for its balanced healing properties and symbolizes growth and renewal

WHAT'S NEXT:

1. Cleanse all your ingredients with sunlight, incense, or the full moon.
2. Put the ingredient in the jar: First the salt; then layer the items from your childhood and the crystals; drop in your blood, herbs/scents, and the honey. Say the following chant three times:

> *"Took my childhood away from me,*
> *I can never have it back;*
> *But with this healing spell,*
> *I will get my life on track again."*

3. Place the lid on and tie the string around it in a bow.
4. Place the jar where you can see. It will remind yourself that you are healing.

Health

This health jar promote physical, emotional, and spiritual health. You may focus on just one intention.

WHAT YOU NEED:

* Jar, bottle, any container that calls to you that you can "seal."
* Herbs. There are many herbs, flowers, and plants associated with healing. My personal favorites are: chamomile, cinnamon, clove, lavender, and rosemary.
* Oil. I like to add a drop of oil either into my bottle, or onto the bottom of the cork before I seal. This is an optional step but can add another element of magic to your spell jar. My favorite oils for good health are: bergamot, lavender, eucalyptus, and sandalwood.
* A candle. I like to seal my spell jars with wax; it allows you to visualize your intention while adding another layer of magic. For health and wellness spells, I almost always use blue or green candles, but white can always be used as a substitute if those aren't available.

WHAT'S NEXT:

1. Start to fill your jar/bottle with each herb. The amount of each is up to you. As you put each herb in, think of its magical properties. Imagine each intention, one on top of the other.
2. Once your jar is full, grab your oil. You can add a drop or two in the jar, or you can anoint the bottom of the cork or lid.
3. Now, grab your candle. Light it, close your eyes, and breathe. Focus your energy, then open your eyes and begin to seal your jar. Please be careful during this step; if you're worried about getting wax on your fingers, place the jar down while sealing (just know that you will most likely make a little mess!)
4. Once your wax is dry, you're done! Hold your jar, visualize the magic inside, feel its power in your hands. So, mote it be.

Home Blessing

This is more a ritual than a classic bottle spell. However, for a home protection spell bottle, find an apothecary bottle or jar with a lid and add the ingredients to it while visualizing your home bathed in a warm protecting energy.

WHAT YOU NEED:

* 4 small jars, without the lids
* 4 small clear crystal quartz to amplify all elements
* Dried white rice for prosperity
* Black salt for purity
* Dried white sage for positive energy
* Dried lavender for peace
* Dried rose petals for love

WHAT'S NEXT:

1. Layer all the ingredients into the 4 jars, starting with the rice.
2. Place your hands-on top of each jar and say:

   "With these elements, I ask for prosperity, purity, positivity, love, and peace for my home and all who live here, and so it is."

3. Repeat for each jar and then place a jar in the North, South, East, and West corner of your home. Do it once a year.

Honey for Making Peace

Honey represents the sweetness with which we face situations.

WHAT YOU NEED:

* A jar of honey
* Two or more grains of rice
* A blue candle (or a pink one)

WHAT'S NEXT:

1. In the waning moon, we place as many grains of rice in the honey jar as there are people with whom we wish to make peace.
2. We light the candle and eat a spoonful of honey, imagining that we will speak kind words to the people we are in conflict with. You must leave the rice in the jar, don't eat it.
3. We leave the grains of rice in honey, and every time we feel the tension, we repeat the ritual again.

Hope

This spell can be used in those periods when you need to be reassured you can handle whatever life throws your way, and everything will be alright.

WHAT YOU NEED:

* Chamomile for calming
* Rose quartz shards for love and trust
* Thyme herb for hope for the future
* Rosemary herb for gentle reassurance
* A sprig of lavender for calming reassurance
* Amethyst shards for hope and power
* Opal shards for calming and hope
* Crushed rose petals for love and trust

WHAT'S NEXT:

1. Layer all the ingredients inside the jar focusing on your intent.
2. Keep it close to you when you need it!

Ignite Love

This is a spell jar to start a loving fire between you and your intent. You will have to put in the work to keep it lit!

WHAT YOU NEED:

* Paper to write the name of your intended
* Bay Leaf for strength, love, and wisdom
* Carnelian for lust, and focus
* Chamomile for happiness, and harmony
* Clove for love, and attraction
* Malachite for fortune, courage, and love
* Pink Himalayan salt for love, and friendship
* Rose oil for joy, peace, energy, love, and gentleness
* Vanilla oil for lust, happiness, and love
* Rose petals for attraction, love, and appreciation
* Rose quartz -for love, and happiness
* Pink wax for love
* Red wax for vitality, love, passion, and initiation

WHAT'S NEXT:

1. Be sure to cleanse your jar. Add as much or as little of the ingredients as you want; keep the paper for last. Then seal with the waxes.

Inner Fire and Energy

WHAT YOU NEED:

* Cinnamon for passion and prosperity
* Ginger for courage and power
* Cloves for power and protection
* Coffee for energy
* Rose for a brave heart
* Orange peels for energy and creativity
* Tiger's eye for protection
* Carnelian for prosperity
* One red or gold candle

WHAT'S NEXT:

1. Take your time to light the candle, meditate, and focus on your intent to awaken the energy inside your soul. Visualize the energy growing within yourself—symbolizing your energy and inner fire.
2. First, add ginger and cinnamon, then layer the other items inside the bottle. Repeat your wish for each item. Add the lid and seal your bottle with wax if you want.
3. Charge the bottle with your intent, and let the jar charge under the light of a full moon.

INNER PEACE

Each ingredient is chosen to bring you harmony and inner peace, to foster tranquility and serenity for yourself and the people around you.

WHAT YOU NEED:

* Lapis lazuli brings deep inner peace, inspires confidence, and helps you speak your truth
* Mullein for grounding and self-assurance
* Calendula for recognizing your worth and ability to flourish, reclaiming boundaries
* Moss to bring protection and connection
* Sodalite helps you to verbalize feelings, calms your mind and eases panic, enhances self-esteem and self-trust
* Lavender relieves stress and brings inner calm
* Jasmine for confidence, self-love, and relief from self-doubt

WHAT'S NEXT:

1. Fill all the ingredients in a bottle and say the following out loud:

   "As I attain this condition of serenity and quiet, I relinquish all stress and fear. I'm at ease, grounded, and centered."

JOB HUNTING

WHAT YOU NEED:

* Sweet orange essential oil for confidence
* Frankincense essential oil to reduce stress and for good luck
* Cinnamon for prosperity, wealth, and a spell booster
* Bay leaf for success, good fortune, achieving a goal, and wishes
* Sage to fulfill wishes
* Black pepper for courage
* Nutmeg for luck and prosperity
* Green candle for money, prosperity, growth, and luck
* Another bay leaf for writing a symbol
* A permanent marker
* Sigil for getting a job

WHAT'S NEXT:

1. Write a symbol on the bay leaf using a permanent marker and charge it by the light of a candle.
2. Then carefully place the materials in the jar and seal it tight using candle wax.

Magical Creativity

WHAT YOU NEED:

* Violet
* Orange peel
* Coffee
* Lavender
* Cinnamon
* Ginger

WHAT'S NEXT:

1. Place the ingredients in the jar and seal it with purple wax.

Memory

Whether it be for finals or just to improve your day-to-day memory, here's a little jar to help you achieve that. Keep it in your pocket, bag, or on your desk or bedside.

WHAT YOU NEED:

* Sea salt for protection
* Rosemary to protect against cellular loss
* Ginkgo biloba to protect against memory loss
* Coffee beans (or powder) to boost cerebral activity
* Sage to help nerves
* Ephedra for energy
* Blue candle

WHAT'S NEXT:

1. Add all the ingredients and seal the jar with blue wax for calmness.
2. Feel free to charge it in the moonlight overnight to strengthen its charge!

Mental and Emotional Health

Healing from any mental or emotional wound can be exhausting, but moving forward is necessary. The unique vibes and metaphysical properties of this blend will support you, encouraging your inner healing.

WHAT YOU NEED:

* Salt for protection, purification
* Cinnamon for protection, speeds up spells, courage
* Rosemary for protection, purification
* Chili flakes to ward off unwanted energies
* Bay for protection against hexes and curses
* Basil for peace, protection, and driving away evil
* Ginger for making spells more powerful, protection
* Black pepper for protection
* Oak leaves for protection, wisdom
* Eggshells for protection

* Lavender for peace, healing, protection
* Sage (please don't use white sage) for protection and purification
* Pen and paper
* Candles: I used a white one and also the wax from my deity candles on my altar

WHAT'S NEXT:

1. As always, ground yourself and cast a circle in the way you prefer.
2. Light all your candles; you can also light some incense if you'd like (in no particular order).
3. Add all your herbs into the jar (using a funnel - even if you make one from paper, it can be really helpful), focusing on intent.
4. Create a sigil with the intent of protection using your own words and method. Draw it on a small slip of paper, fold and add to the jar.
5. Speak affirmations into the jar focusing on the protection of yourself (or whoever will be wearing this). You can also repeat the statement used for the sigil.
6. Put the lid on and place the jar on something you can pour the candle wax onto.
7. Pour all the candle wax onto your spell jar, allowing it to run down the sides and even create a pool at the bottom.
8. Allow the candle wax to mainly dry and remove the bottle. It is now done. I like to put the leftover wax that's not attached on a wax melt thingy and melt it for further protection.

MENTAL CLARITY

This particular spell jar helps with keeping a clear and focused mind, while encouraging effective communication and decision making. It can also be kept out while studying, reading, or doing any activity that requires mental focus.

WHAT YOU NEED:

* Mint for communication
* Rosemary to improve efficiency, memory retention, positively affect cognitive performance
* Cinnamon for protection and mental focus
* Ground coffee to dispel negative thoughts
* Sea salt for protection and cleansing
* Agrimony for overcoming fear and inner blockages
* Basil to dispel confusion, fears, and weaknesses
* Frankincense oil to reduce hyperactivity, impatience, irritability, and restlessness
* Peppermint oil to invigorate the mind, improve memory, and provide insight
* Yellow wax

WHAT'S NEXT:

1. Layer the ingredients while concentrating your purpose.
2. Seal using yellow wax for brainpower, focus, concentration, intellect, and memory improvement.

Money and Prosperity

The money jar spell is a powerful way to draw money to you. Use this jar if you're ever in a pinch or use it as a continuous way to attract money into your home or business. Best performed on a Sunday (prosperity, health, and overall success) at midday (health, money, and success) and during a waxing moon (growth, attraction, production, power, and creation).

WHAT YOU NEED:
  * Cinnamon for money, luck, success, prosperity
  * Marjoram for wealth, happiness, protection
  * Oregano for action, courage, energy
  * Basil for prosperity, success, wealth, happiness
  * Clove for prosperity, protection
  * Thyme for luck, prosperity, health
  * Gold glitter for luck, prosperity, money
  * Copper penny/silver dime
  * Green wax for accumulating money and wealth and promoting prosperity and abundance

WHAT'S NEXT:
  1. Fill the jar with the herb and glitter ingredients one at a time while focusing on your intention.
  2. Next, place an old copper penny or silver dime in the jar. Seal and store the jar.

Motivation

Do you have the workweek blues? Or perhaps you just need a nudge to get things done. Keep yourself feeling positive with this easy spell bottle.

WHAT YOU NEED
  * Chicory root to remove obstacles
  * Coffee for energy, grounding, inspiring
  * Cinnamon for success, energy
  * Bay leaf for wishes, goals, manifesting
  * Rosemary for focus, cleansing
  * Mint for freshness, strength
  * Lemon balm for balance, eases anxiety, aids in problem-solving
  * Tiger's eye for courage, motivation, energy
  * Orange candle for motivation, ambition, success

WHAT'S NEXT
  1. To begin spell work, ground and center yourself, draw a circle, summon the quarters, doing whatever you typically do.
  2. To create this ritual bottle, begin by cleansing the bottle, the place you're working in, and yourself with rosemary or sage. Make a little piece of paper to fit the base of your bottle by tracing it and cutting it out.

3. On this bit of paper, create a spiral symbol and anoint it with peppermint or rosemary essential oil. The spiral sign represents life, vitality, and spiritual growth. It will aid in amplifying the magic bottle's motivating energy. Set a goal for yourself using this spell. What does drive mean to you, and how will you begin to be more fruitful? Consider an occasion when you were inspired. Where did you get your motivated energy?

4. Then, beginning with the spiral sign, put each component into your magic bottle with purpose. You may recite aloud each thing you're putting into your magic bottle and the function it provides to this spell if you choose. Cover it with the wax of an orange candle after all of the objects have been inserted. You may anoint the candle and etch the spiral symbol or perhaps the word "inspiration" into it before lighting it.

5. Once the magic bottle is sealed, light some rosemary and run it through the smoke, saying:

   "Air to motivate."

6. Then pass it over the flame of the candle, saying:

   "Fire to give desire.
   Motivation, attention, and determination flow through me."

7. Recite your magic aloud over a tarot card (indicating discoveries, clarity, and opportunity).

8. Allow 3 hours for your magic bottle to charge in the sun on top of the tarot card. Keep your magic bottle wherever you'll see it on a regular basis. When you need a boost of inspiration, give it a bounce or keep it in your hands. Try sitting with it outside in the sun.

ᛟERVOUSNESS

For those of you looking for a witchy boost to help with your nervousness and anxiety. Perhaps also useful for those of you shaken by a recent event.

WHAT YOU NEED:
* Black tea for strength, fortitude
* Amethyst tumble stones for healing the mind, peace
* Rosemary for cleansing, restoring focus and memory
* Coffee power booster to dispel negative thoughts and for grounding
* Valerian for harmony
* Rose quartz tumble stones for peace and self-love
* Catnip for cheerfulness and love
* Bay leaf for petitioning/wishing
* Paper and pen
* Incense (a calming one for you)
* White candle

WHAT'S NEXT:
1. For a relaxing atmosphere, light some incense and a white candle. Make a list of your concerns and anxieties using a bit of paper and a pen. Allow the ashes to fall into the jar after lighting the piece of paper with a white candle.

2. In the jar containing the ashes, combine the black tea, amethyst, rosemary, coffee, valerian, rose quartz, catnip, and bay leaf.

3. Allow the smoke to permeate the crystals by standing over them. Say this statement three times as you go.

> *"You are no longer alive, nervous anxiousness.*
> *May the goods listed below help me to relax.*
> *Bring me your tranquility.*
> *Blessed be, you will no longer have anxiety thoughts."*

No More Nightmares

This jar spell is created to get rid of nightmares and help you sleep soundly, protecting you from unwanted thoughts while calming your mind before sleep.

WHAT YOU NEED:
* Sea salt to purify and heal the mind, ensuring good dreams
* Anise star: Wards off nightmares
* Lavender for deep and peaceful sleep
* Jasmine to promote calming energies and relaxation
* Amethyst chips to emit a calming vibration to facilitate a deep sleep
* Rose quartz chips to alleviate negative emotions that prevent restful sleep

WHAT'S NEXT:
1. Seal with white wax and charge the jar in whatever way you please to ensure its power.
2. Sleep with the jar under your pillow or beside your head to ensure a restful sleep and good dreams!

Online Exams

WHAT YOU NEED:
* Coffee beans and instant coffee for concentration and energy
* Popcorn kernels and dried assorted flower seeds for potential
* Carraway seeds for mental fortitude
* Thyme for protection and comfort
* Cinnamon for creativity
* Orange star sequins/orange fake flower for academic success and creativity
* Dried Daffodil petals for academic success
* Bay leaves for personal strength
* Whole cloves for happiness
* Amber and clear quartz shards for concentration, and mental clarity
* Tag Locks

WHAT'S NEXT:
1. Layer all the ingredients in your jar and place it next to you during the exam.

Good Vibes Only

A little jar to cleanse your energy while replacing it with a lighter, positive one.

WHAT YOU NEED:

* Sea salt
* Citrus peel to signify the sun
* Rosemary, often used in sage bundles to cleanse a home
* Eucalyptus for healing, protection, and fresh energy
* Wormwood for protection, and send negativity back to the sender
* Vervain for cleansing your spaces, stagnant energies, and auras
* Juniper berries for purification, and protection
* Sage as a major negativity banisher
* White candle to promote positive energy
* Black candle to banish negativity
* Orange/yellow wax or a ribbon to seal the jar
* Citrine, tourmaline, and aura quartz, (optional, and to charge your bottle)

WHAT'S NEXT:

1. Focus your energy on the herbs as you put them in your jar, and as you are doing so, envision a big ball of light surrounding yourself.
2. Seal the jar with orange wax or a ribbon.
3. Charge the jar and crystals in the sunlight.

Overthinking and Worry

When life gets too much and I start to get trapped into my negative loop, I need to have something calm to focus on and center myself. I only hope it can help some of you too.

WHAT YOU NEED:

* Rosemary for love, long life, happiness
* Marjoram for harmony, peace, tranquility
* Cloves for healing
* Lavender for dispelling depression and for healing and peace
* Sandalwood oil for meditation
* Blue bluebell-scented wax for sealing
* Blue glitter

WHAT'S NEXT:

1. I sealed the jar with blue bluebell-scented wax after combining the herbs, oil, and glitter.
2. I chose blue wax because it symbolizes freedom, sensitivity, and faith.
3. I chose candles that were bluebell-scented because bluebells symbolize humility and constancy.
4. The blue glitter was a bonus because, quite frankly, I don't think glitter has ever made anything worse before. Also, it's very, very pretty.

Peace and Positivity at Home

Place this spell bottle somewhere visible to act as a reminder to strengthen the intentions you have with a happy home.

WHAT YOU NEED:

* Jasmine flowers for prosperity and harmony
* Chrysanthemum for protection and blessings
* Lavender for happiness, peace of mind, and harmony
* Roses for protection, luck, confidence, and trust
* Basil for peace and protection
* Cinnamon stick for prosperity and protection
* Clove with a red string for protection
* Sea salt for protection
* Clear Quartz crystal to absorb negativity. It is a good energy booster.
* Sodalite stone to balance emotions

WHAT'S NEXT:

1. Cleanse and charge the items under the full moon
2. Light your candle and fill the jar with your ingredients. Chant the following 3 times while you do so:

   "I want to invoke the safety of this gorgeous moon over myself, my house, and my loved.
   I embrace the moon's energy as a source of power for myself and my household.
   Negative energy and people will abandon my house and heart because they are not welcome.
   There is nothing except peace.
   So, it shall be."

3. Tie the clove around the jar with a red string 3 times.

Pet Protection

Animals are more than just our best friends; they are part of our souls and complete our lives.

WHAT YOU NEED:

* Candle wax
* Salt
* Pine needles
* Taglock (A pet's hair, or a feather, a lost tooth/nail, etc.)
* Rosemary
* Juniper
* Eggshell powder

WHAT'S NEXT:

4. Combine all components in a bottle except the taglock and sigil.
5. On a bit of paper, write your objectives and then draw a sigil on top of them. Use your chosen way to activate the symbol (but don't destroy it).

6. Fold the paper as many times as you can, and tuck it into the taglock.
7. Place the paper and tag lock in the jar and repeat three times,

"(Target's name) is safe from any harm across their life."

8. Use candle wax to seal the container.

PHOEBE'S LUCK

WHAT YOU NEED:

* Amethyst for protection
* Shell for life
* Rose quartz for love
* Lavender for purity
* Cinnamon for healing
* Pink salt for prosperity

WHAT'S NEXT:

1. Hold the bottle in both hands and fill it with your aspirations and dreams. Say:

"On this planet, I utilize my energy to promote love and happiness, which has blessed me with the capacity to flourish and aid others."

2. Never trade the bottle, and use the chant to fill it with your monthly objectives.

POSITIVE INTENTIONS

WHAT YOU NEED:

* Bay leaf
* Thyme
* Sage
* Mint
* Lavender
* Basil
* Rosemary
* Paper and pen
* Burning dish
* Candle

WHAT'S NEXT:

1. Set positive intentions while adding the bay leaf, sage, thyme, mint, basil, lavender, and rosemary in the bottle.
2. Fill the blanks on a little piece of paper with your objectives. In a flaming dish, char the paper. Fill the bottle with the ashes. Use wax to close the bottle.
3. Carry it with you to offer relaxing energy.

Productive Energy

This spell is for enhancing your productive energy when you feel a bit off.

WHAT YOU NEED:

* Yellow candle for productive energy to seal jar
* Cinnamon or cayenne pepper for success and energy
* Black pepper to enhance energy
* Crushed ped pepper to enhance energy
* Dried lavender for healing and calming
* Dragon's blood calcite/red calcite to enhance energy and grounding (optional)

WHAT'S NEXT:

1. Layer the ingredients, filling each with intent and energy.
2. Once you're done layering, seal the jar with the wax from the yellow candle.
3. Crystals of your choice can be used to enhance the intention while you're creating the spell jar.
4. Meditate with it for a few minutes.

Productivity and Motivation

It encourages you to be in the present moment and helps you stay motivated. Place it on your desk or carry one in your pocket/ to enhance productivity.

WHAT YOU NEED:

* Kosher Salt to absorb residual negativity
* Black Pepper to banish bad habits and emotions that hinder me
* Peppermint for energy
* Coffee for motivation
* Cinnamon for success and prosperity
* Rosemary to improve memory.
* Eye drops to improve focus and clarity.

WHAT'S NEXT:

1. Light some candles and whip up this little jar to give a boost.

Prosperity Charm

A simple spell to draw in good things and grant general prosperity. Charms function best when they're used with a clear aim, so bless it and keep it nearby! And observe as your life blooms with success!

WHAT YOU NEED:

* Dried rose petals for kind feelings in life
* Cinnamon for wealth and prosperity
* White sugar to bring good-natured things to you

* Pink Himalayan rock salt for defense against negativity
* Dried coffee grounds for motivation and as a catalyst
* Rose quartz - optional

WHAT'S NEXT:

1. Charge with rose quartz or sunlight, seal with a kiss.

Prosperity Jar

This prosperity jar spell focuses on thriving economically rather than being generally successful.

WHAT YOU NEED:

* Sea salt for protection
* Basil for money, wealth
* Rosemary for mental clarity
* Tigers Eye for additional protection (or, you can use gem chips and charge them next to a tiger eye)
* Green wax for wealth and luck

WHAT'S NEXT:

2. Layer starting with salt about a quarter way full.
3. Then add the basil, rosemary, and Tigers Eye chips while focusing your intention.
4. Charge it with your intention for wealth and luck, and you're good to go!

Protect Your Love Relationship

The best place for this love blessing bottle is in the bedroom or some other intimate area where love flows freely.

WHAT YOU NEED:

* Sprigs of lavender to encourage a peaceful and calm environment
* Roses and rose quartz crystals to encourage self-love and love in relationships
* Jasmine flowers to attract any kind of wealth
* Hibiscus flowers to attract lust and love. It has a strong connection with the divine feminine
* Heather flowers to encourage easy communication
* A bay leaf for protection
* Damiana, an aphrodisiac
* Rose oil to increase magical and physical energy, sex, and love
* White candle

WHAT'S NEXT:

1. Bless all of the herbs within with rose oil.
2. Both of you, take the jar and fill it with the ingredients, both focusing on the intent of the jar.
3. Seal it with white candle wax. The candle on top is included to give energy to the jar as well when it's lit.

PROTECTION

This little yet powerful jar will guard you against negative influences and protect you mentally, physically, and spiritually.

WHAT YOU NEED:

* Frankincense incense
* Salt for protection, purification
* Cinnamon for protection, speeds up spells, courage
* Rosemary for protection, purification
* Chili flakes to ward off unwanted energies
* Basil for peace and protection
* Ginger to make the spell more powerful
* Black pepper for protection
* Oak leaves for protection and wisdom
* Eggshells for protection
* Lavender for peace and healing
* Sage for protection, and purification
* Paper and pen
* Small amethyst
* Small obsidian
* Candles: I used a white one and also the wax from the deity candles on my altar

WHAT'S NEXT:

1. With the paper and pen, create a sigil for protection.
2. Light the candle and incense.
3. Hold the jar over the candle.
4. Tip the jar over and hold it, opening over the incense. Fill the jar with smoke.
5. Add all the ingredients (If using a small jar, you may want to grind the herbs and use a funnel to get them into the opening)
6. Add your sigil to the jar and close it.
7. Cover the opening of the jar with wax from the candle.
8. Snuff the candle. It can be used for future protection jars.
9. Place your protection jar somewhere safe, or bury it near whatever you are protecting.

PROTECTION AND LUCK

This jar is excellent at attracting luck of all kinds, especially wealth and wish-granting; it works really well for protection against ill intentions and helps curb bad energy. I love this easy spell because you can find everything you need in your kitchen!

WHAT YOU NEED:

* Ground nutmeg for grounding, good luck, stability, household funds, protection of wealth
* Garlic seeds for home and financial stability, prosperity, productivity, opportunities, in-

tention setting, financial growth and protection, psychic protection, and intuition

* Oregano for abundance, communication, growth of wealth, prosperity, career luck, and encourages happiness
* Dried moss for household stability, financial stability, connection to earth, love, grounding
* Whole clove(s) for protection, abundance, stability, growth, prosperity, manifestation, energy, and good luck
* Black peppercorns for protection, motivation, banishing negative energies, stability, and grounding
* Dried bay leaf (crumbled) for intuition, wish-granting, communication, good luck, abundance, good energies, financial protection, psychic protection

WHAT'S NEXT:

1. Cleanse your jar and space, and empower it with your intent.
2. Gather all your ingredients together, and add them to the jar.
3. Once you're happy with the jar, go ahead and close it.
4. After you feel the spell has done its job, you can choose to recharge it or dispose of it, whichever feels right to you.

Protection Charm

To offer extra protection to the wearer from bad energies. It can also be placed over windows and doors, keeping your home, work, or wherever needed safe and protected.

You can add selenite for an extra boost. It is a fantastic tool for shifting those energy blocks that stop you from living in your full and fluid flow.

WHAT YOU NEED:

* Protective herbs/plants of your choice
* Pine
* Salt
* Bay leaves
* Sewing pins
* Selenite (optional)
* Candle
* Sharpie

WHAT'S NEXT:

1. Place all of the herbs and plants in the bottle after you've gathered them all; it doesn't matter which order things go in.
2. Last, put the pins in the container, imagining a protective sphere surrounding yourself.
3. Once it's all in the bottle, close it up, very cautiously—it's possible to burn yourself or drop hot wax!
4. Bind the charm by pouring wax from the candle down the edge of cork or the top. Say,
   "By the light of the sun,
   on this foggy night,
   I call upon kindness to give me your strength,
   By the strength of 3,
   this will defend me."

Planetary Charm Jars

Create one of these jars to represent whichever planet you choose! You can use it as offerings, spell components, or altar display.

BASIC INGREDIENTS:
Glitter | Sea Salt | Essential oil | Gem chips | Small jar

Planetary Variants:

MOON
White glitter
Sea salt
Lemon essential oil
Clear or milky quartz

SUN
Gold glitter
Sea salt
Orange essential oil
Citrine

MERCURY
Yellow glitter
Sea salt
Eucalyptus essential oil
Aventurine

VENUS
Pink glitter
Himalayan pink salt
Rose essential oil
Rose quartz

MARS
Red glitter
Sea salt or red salt
Cinnamon essential oil
Red agate

JUPITER
Blue glitter
Sea salt
Sage essential oil
Amethys

SATURN
Purple glitter
Sea salt or black salt
Cypress essential oil
Garnet

URANUS
Light blue glitter
Sea salt
Lime essential oil
Clear quartz

NEPTUNE
Dark blue glitter
Sea salt
Jasmine essential oil
Aquamarine

PLUTO
Black glitter
Black salt
Basil essential oil
Onyx

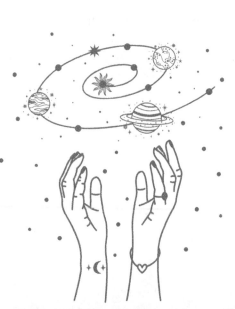

Protection Powder

This blend of herbs is super versatile and brings the strength of fire to protect you and your home.

WHAT YOU NEED*:*

* Black salt protects and absorbs negativity
* Black pepper for protection, banishment - fire element
* Basil for protection, and peace - fire element
* Cayenne pepper for protection - fire element
* Chili powder heightens spell power and protect
* Cinnamon for prosperity, and peace- fire element
* Clove for protection, and banishment - fire element
* Thorns for extra punishment, and protection.
* Clear quartz to amplify the strength of the spell
* Black tourmaline for stronger protection

WHAT'S NEXT:

1. Mix all the ingredients in a little jar. Have a specific intent in mind while you add. Something like:

   "Protect me and my space from harmful intruders."

2. There are two ways you can use this magic mix. You can keep the jar inside your house. Alternatively, you can leave out the crystals and thorns and sprinkle the protection powder around the edge of your home.

Psychic Enhancement

This jar is strong! You could use it to help your astral travel, add power to a spell, to help speak with spirits—anything you want.

WHAT YOU NEED:

* A four-leaf clover for psychic power
* Basil herb for magical power
* Sage protection and psychic power
* Amethyst shards for magikcal power
* Sea salt for protection and power
* Rosemary herb for magical power
* Tiger's eye shards for empowerment
* Carnelian shards for energy
* A quartz point to enhance your intent
* A key-like metal object to unlock your ability

WHAT'S NEXT:

1. Place the ingredients in the jar while focusing on your intent.

PURIFICATION

A special blend of herbs to help in cleansing, clearing, and purifying. It can also be added to purification and cleansing rituals and spells to help hold the initial intention.

WHAT YOU NEED:
* Salt
* Cinnamon for protection, speeds up spells, courage
* Rosemary for protection, purification
* Chili flakes for warding off unwanted energies
* Bay for protection against hexes and curses
* Basil for peace, protection, and to drive away evil
* Ginger for making spells more powerful, protection
* Black pepper for protection
* Oak leaves for protection, wisdom
* Eggshells for protection
* Lavender for peace, healing, protection
* Sage for protection, purification
* Paper
* Pen
* Spell bottle jar
* Candles

WHAT'S NEXT:
1. As usual, ground yourself and cast a circle, and light all your candles in no particular sequence; you may even burn incense if you'd like.
2. Fill the jar with all of your herbs (using a funnel, even if it's made of paper, may be quite beneficial), focusing on purpose.
3. With your own words and manner, design a sigil with the intention of protection.
4. Draw it on a little piece of paper, fold it in half, and place it in the jar. Speak affirmations into the jar, concentrating on your own safety.
5. You may also say the sigil's statement again. Place the lid on the jar and set it on a surface where you can drip the candle wax.
6. Pour all of the candle wax into the magic jar, allowing it to drip down the sides and form a pool at the base.
7. Remove the container once the candle wax has mostly dried. It has now been completed. I prefer to melt the wax from the leftover wax that isn't connected to a wax melt item for added protection.

REASSURANCE

Reassurance spell jar for anyone needing to get rid of doubts and fears during tough times! It only needs to be set with the right intent! Keep it in your bag, pocket, or on your desk or bedside. Anywhere near you when you need that reassurance. Feel free to charge it in the moonlight overnight when received to strengthen its charge!

WHAT YOU NEED:
* White candle for peace
* Paper and pen
* Obsidian to dispel negative energy
* Citrine for healing (If you prefer not to use citrine because it is heat-treated amethyst, that is fine. Amethyst can be substituted in for its calming abilities)
* Salt for protection
* Basil for love and protection
* Parsley for love and protection
* Rosemary for healing
* Thyme for healing
* Turmeric for purification

WHAT'S NEXT:
1. Begin by grabbing your pen, paper, and obsidian. Hold the obsidian in your hand as you think of a phrase of protection. Mine was, "*I am safe, there is no pain here.*"
2. With the obsidian in your hand write the phrase on the paper. Let the energy from your obsidian dispel any negative thoughts. When you're finished, roll it into a size that will fit into your bottle.
3. Prepare your other ingredients. Let each herb touch the citrine. Let them absorb the citrine's healing power. Layer in your salt, basil, parsley, rosemary, thyme, and turmeric into the bottle. Somewhere halfway through, place your rolled note into the bottle and let it be covered.
4. Close your bottle and light a white candle. Gently wave your bottle over the smoke for purification, then use the melted wax to seal your bottle.
5. Keep the finished spell bottle somewhere you can easily and quickly find it. On its own it will fill whatever room or space it's placed in with positive energy.
6. Whenever you feel extra anxious or upset, grab the bottle, and hold it in your hands. Repeat the phrase written inside the bottle while breathing deeply. Let the phrase and the love from the bottle lift you up. Repeat as often as needed.

℞EMEMBER YOUR 𝔇REAMS

WHAT YOU NEED:
* A white or purple candle
* Mugwort to remember dreams/vivid dreams
* Lavender for peaceful and healthy sleep
* Lemongrass for protection from nightmares

WHAT'S NEXT:
1. Light your candle while visualizing with your intent.
2. Add the ingredients in the following order: mugwort, lavender, and lemongrass.
3. Keep it beside your bed at night, it should help! I would still advise writing dreams down when you can remember.
4. This jar can also be charged whenever you feel you need the boost!
5. Happy dreaming!

RISE PERSONAL POWER

This powerful spell is designed to increase the effectiveness of your own spell workings and channel your personal power and strength in any area of life. perform this spell on a Friday or during a waxing moon.

WHAT YOU NEED:

* Cinnamon for prophetic dreams
* Ginger for strength and speed of your work
* Basil for protection and to drive off any negativity
* Marjoram for protection
* Sage and black salt for protection
* Myrrh resin to enhance psychic vibrations
* Wormwood to enhance divinatory abilities
* Uva ursi for increasing psychic and intuitive powers
* Mugwort to bring about prophetic dreams and increase power
* Dandelion for psychic guidance
* Amethyst crystal to develop psychic powers and intuition
* Lotus incense for mental clarity, focus, and heightened intelligence

WHAT'S NEXT:

1. Cleanse your altar or kitchen space.
2. Add the mint, chamomile, thyme, sage, and lavender one at a time to the jar. Focus on letting positivity infuse the mixture and say,

   "May this mix bring intuition, positivity,
   and balance to my life.
   May this mix ward against negativity,
   And banish any strife.
   May this mix enhance my psychic abilities,
   and strengthen my magic work."

3. Seal the jar and give it a good shake.
4. Burn the incense in an open fire.

SAFETY BOOST

Place this little jar in your window for an extra boost of safety. It is super cute to boot and very easy to make.

WHAT YOU NEED:

* Markers or paint in white, black, and blue (or any color you like)
* Herbs that you use for protection (I used arnica flowers, agrimony, thyme, pennyroyal, juniper berries, and a few others)
* Sandalwood, patchouli, dragons' blood, or sage incense to purify
* Sigils you use for protection

WHAT'S NEXT:

1. Draw a blue eye on the jar and let it dry. The blue eye is traditional, but you can use any color that feels safe.
2. Paint on the jar any protection sigils, and let it dry.
3. Now, it is time to open a circle if you wish so.
4. Layer in the herbs or mix them all.
5. Purify and bless the jar with incense.
6. Keep this jar on a window sill or hanging in a window. Turn the eye outward so it can watch out for bad energies that could come your way.

SELF–EMPOWERMENT

This bottle spell is for everyone who needs a little more confidence, a little more badassery, a bit more self-love.

WHAT YOU NEED:

* Thyme herb for strength
* Rosemary herb for mental power and courage
* Crushed bay leaf for protection
* Sage herb for protection and strength
* Sea salt for protection and healing
* Garnet shards for self-love, raw power, and tough skin

WHAT'S NEXT:

1. Place the ingredients in the jar while focusing on your intent.

SELF–LOVE

It is pointless to craft a self-love jar if you are in a negative frame of mind. Remember, you get what you put. Put on your favorite music, dance around, or do something you enjoy to get yourself in a good mood.

WHAT YOU NEED:

* Brown sugar to add a little sweetness.
* Rose petals for attracting things to you, and beauty spells too.
* Black salt to protect and purify.
* Lavender to calm and improve awareness. Also, to rid anxiety.
* Rose quartz to create feelings of peace and open your heart.
* Hibiscus flowers, great for attraction and helping with dreams.
* Rosemary, a perfect substitute for any herb; it is my go-to herb for many rituals and spells. It stops gossip and is great for memory.
* Sage leaves for writing your mantra or intentions.
* Pink peppercorns to push you a little.
* Cinnamon to get rid of negative energy and awaken your power!
* Pink candle to seal the jar.

WHAT'S NEXT:

1. Light your favorite relaxing incense and take a few deep breaths before placing all your items into a jar.
2. While adding each item, say what you wish to gain or are wanting from the item. For example: ***"I add lavender to give me a sense of calm and ease my anxiety."***
3. I like to write clear directions with a permanent marker on the bay leaves.
   "I am strong,
   I love my body..."
4. After you have added all of the items, seal the spell with the candle. Light it and let the wax drip down the sides of the jar.
5. While the wax is still wet, place the rose quartz into the wax.
6. Hold the jar tight in your hands and feel the positivity you just created.
7. Place it on your altar or bedside table, or anywhere else you see it regularly.

Self–Love for Your Friends

Everyone wants their friends to be loved and happy; here's a way to send them self-love in a bottle.

WHAT YOU NEED:

* Sea salt
* Cinnamon
* Apple pie spice
* Black tea
* Epsom salt
* Lavender
* Rosemary
* Rose petals
* White rose petals
* Dandelion wishes
* Sunflower
* Vanilla oil

WHAT'S NEXT:

1. Layer the ingredients in this order: Sea salt, cinnamon, apple pie spice, black tea, Epsom salt, lavender, rosemary, rose petals, white rose petals, dandelion, and sunflower.
2. Then, add three drops of vanilla saying:
   "Love yourself as I love you. This spell will take away your blue. See yourself the way you truly are. Self-love is what's contained within this jar."
3. Sprinkle some sugar (optional) and then seal your jar.

Self–Transformation

This spell is best performed during Summer Solstice/full moon. Be and make it all about your new beginnings! Keep in mind I created this bottle in relation to huge changes in my life and what I needed help with at the moment. It can easily be altered to focus on your troubles.

WHAT YOU NEED:

* Salt
* Used coffee grounds for promoting productivity and banishing bad habits (I used coffee grounds from the pot of coffee I shared with my husband that morning to symbolize his support and love)

* Rosemary for intellectual improvement
* Sage for healing, both mental and physical
* Thyme for change and transformation
* Basil for expelling negativity
* Parsley for strength, vitality, and passion
* Apple stems (for personal and magical growth)
* Cinnamon stick for healing and passion
* Dried rose petals as a reminder of all the love in my life that I sometimes forget
* Quartz for spiritual growth and development
* Tiger's eye for willpower, prosperity, and courage
* A red ribbon for passion, enthusiasm, energy, strength and courage

WHAT'S NEXT:

1. While adding the ingredients, chant:

   "I will persevere,
   I will overcome myself,
   I will conquer my demons."

2. I first added dried, used coffee grounds and salt to the jar.
3. Next, I blended and added the herbs, apple stems, and cinnamon sticks (you can also use ground cinnamon).
4. Finally, I topped it off with the dried rose petals and the crystals.
5. I "sealed" it with the red ribbon and charged it for a few hours in the sunlight.

SLEEPING

WHAT YOU NEED:

* Amethyst
* Cinnamon
* Lavender
* Holy basil
* Thyme
* Bay leaf or paper to write sigils/runes for peace

WHAT'S NEXT:

1. Cleanse the bag and materials as you prefer.
2. Simply toss the materials inside the bottle.
3. Tuck it under the pillow or in the bed at night.

REDUCE PUBLIC SPEAKING ANXIETY

Sometimes presentations and other forms of public speaking can be terrifying. I can't even speak in front of a small group of people without shaking and stuttering. This jar will help you cope with that fear and bring about a sense of calm and confidence in these situations.

WHAT YOU NEED:

* Sugar to sweeten any challenge

* Clovers for knowledge and luck
* Pine cones for memory and helping you stay on track
* Amethyst, or any other crystal to calm anxiety
* Turquoise, or any other crystal for communication
* Orange candle for excitement or call to action
* Something you have a personal connection with to provide comfort. For me, this was fern, since I'm drawn to the forest and go there often

WHAT'S NEXT:

1. Add everything in a bottle and seal with wax of the candle.

Spiritual Grounding

WHAT YOU NEED:

* 4 rose buds
* Lavender
* Chamomile
* Jasmine
* Ground clove
* Ground cinnamon
* Olive oil
* Amethyst

WHAT'S NEXT:

1. Add everything in a bottle and seal with wax of the candle.

Spiritual Protection

Where did this spell come from? Through my growth, I've come to understand my energy, my control of it, and the influence that other people might have on all of it. This jar wants to protect you from all the negative emotions and feelings these people may cause.

WHAT YOU NEED:

* Pink Himalayan Salt for cleansing, purifying, and charging your intent
* Poppy seeds offer respect to spirits and sets a tone of understanding of the spiritual realm. Red rose petals to uplift the spirit, raise vibrations, protect, and empower
* Rose stems and thorns to defends and brings confidence
* Cedar or sage ash - the ashes of any cleansing tool will do
* Amethyst to protect the body, mind, and your dream spaces
* Quartz to bring power and positive energy to your intent
* White wax to cleanse, protect, and reflect thus amplify our intent

WHAT'S NEXT:

1. Light the candle. Close your eyes, breathe deeply for a couple of minutes focusing on your intent.
2. Add each ingreditnts calling its purpose, and use the white wax to seal.
3. Keep it close to you whenever you need an extra boost of protection.

Stop Procrastination!

A spell designed to help minimize procrastination and encourage hard work and focus.

~

WHAT YOU NEED:

Herbs, use at least two:
Lavender for clarity of thought
Rue for clearness of mind, ridding of emotional stress
Thyme to keep away negative energy
Rosemary for improved clarity, increases concentration
Basil for relief from mental fatigue, aid in mental fortitude
White or blue candle
Crystals, not mandatory but can be used to help refine your intent: Clear quartz, selenite, fluorite

~

WHAT'S NEXT:

Optional - Charge the dried herbs in the sun for at least half an hour. I always relate the sun to energy, so it should help streighten their effect.

Light the candle, and sprinkle a bit of salt over the herbs for protection; while doing this, say:

"I ask you to protect me from the negative thoughts that prevent me from my work."

Begin filling your jar with the herbs; as you put an herb in, state its intent and what you want it to do for the spell. Repeat this for all the herbs you add. The jar should not be filled entirely.

After all the herbs are in, pour the salt that you sprinkled over the herbs in and restate that you want it to protect you.

Hold your now filled-with-herbs jar out in front of you and say the following:

"Help me keep my goal in mind,
Make it so I complete in time,
Do not let me be swayed,
Help me focus,
And keep my thoughts in place."

After you finish the chant, place your thumb over the top of the jar and give the contents a good couple of shakes while keeping the thoughts "help me focus" in mind.

After this, you can cork your jar, use the wax from your candle to seal.

SWEET DREAMS

WHAT YOU NEED:

* Chamomile
* Thyme
* Amethyst
* Jasmine
* Lavender
* Purple Candle

WHAT'S NEXT:

1. Your candle should be lit.
2. Combine all of the ingredients in a bottle.
3. Recite the following spell 3 times while doing so:

"The moon is my companion.
Keeping an eye on me.
Bringing the splendor of nature into my dreams.
The stars will continue to shine forever.
Bringing calm and tranquility to the mind.
They won't leave when I shut my eyes, keeping me secure till the light."

SWEETENING

WHAT YOU NEED:

* 1 pink candle
* Honey
* Paper
* Pen or pencil
* One of these herbs: bay leaf, lavender, cinnamon

WHAT'S NEXT:

1. Write the person's complete name on the sheet of paper. Sprinkle a bit of the herb of your choice on top of the paper (Purifying and protecting properties are found in bay leaf, lavender, and cinnamon).
2. Fold the paper in half and insert it into the jar. Toss a teaspoon of honey into the container. Add an additional spoonful until the paper is completely covered.
3. Tightly close the jar. Ignite the candle and position it on top of the lid.
4. Say the following magic to yourself, feel free to say what you want to banish from this person:

"Love, sweetness, self-love, calmness."

5. Visualize the person's attitude toward you sweetening as you concentrate on the lit candle. Imagine someone who is kind, smiling, and caring about you.

UNBINDING

This little but whoppingly powerful spell will burn away all bindings from a persona that has kept you stuck and prevented you from moving forward.

WHAT YOU NEED:

*   A picture of the person you are unbinding from yourself
*   Two scrolls of paper with your names on each one
*   A string
*   Red chili flakes, used for banishing negativity
*   Table salt to cleanse and purify
*   Black candle to banish bad energy
*   White candle to purify
*   An artifact that symbolizes your friendship

WHAT'S NEXT:

1. On one scrap of paper, write your name, while on the other, specify the other person's name. Using a length of thread, attach the two pieces of paper.
2. Place a black candle on the table. Burn the thread linking the papers with your objective in mind (amputating the link between the 2 of you).
3. Rip the person's photo apart. Burn the image and the paper slips slowly and gently.
4. Fill your jar with the ashes, then add red chili flakes and salt.
5. Optional: I included a ring that she handcrafted for me in my jar.
6. Place the white candle on the table. Close the jar with white candle wax, bearing your objective in mind (closing off the jar and hence banishing and breaking your relationship).

UNLOCK DOORS

This spell will help you open doors to new opportunities and experiences that will lead you to meet new people, a source of income, or evolve as a person.

WHAT YOU NEED:

*   Basil for luck
*   Rosemary or sage for protection
*   Lavender to reduce anxieties
*   Strawberry leaf for success and fortune
*   Bay leaf for wishes
*   Lemongrass to repel evil from your path
*   Spearmint for money, passionflower for friendship
*   Angelica root for blessings
*   Green glitter for growth
*   Black glitter for protection
*   Blue glitter for a sense of wanderlust and optimism
*   Orange glitter for success and opening the roads ahead

* Orange candle for ambition, and opportunity
* Purple candle for driving away evil, and wisdom

WHAT'S NEXT:

1. I didn't create a specific incantation, but along with verbalizing the purpose of each ingredient and item used, I wrote on a piece of paper what I wanted from this spell jar and added it before I sealed my jar.

WISDOM AND WIT

Are you looking for insights? This bottle spell will bring you wisdom and knowledge by connecting through the spiritual realm. Meditation and mantras work effectively together to fulfill the intention of this little jar.

WHAT YOU NEED:

* Lavender for psychic powers and clarity
* Sage for wisdom
* Peppermint for mental strength
* Parsley to reveal the truth
* Lemon balm for foresight
* Nut powder for intelligence
* Amethyst for vision, intuition, and enhancing psychic abilities
* Jasmine for psychic powers
* Acorn for wisdom
* A candle: purple, blue or silver

WHAT'S NEXT:

1. Take your time to light a candle, meditate, and focus on your intent.
2. Visualize energy growing within yourself, symbolizing your mind awakening and power.
3. Add all the ingredients, finishing with the amethyst. Repeat your wish for each item.
4. Finally, add the lid and seal the bottle with the candle's wax.
5. Charge the bottle with your intent. It is like adding a layer of energy.
6. Charge under the moonlight (better during the last quarter).
7. Carry the jar with you to perceive the truth and use it to make important decisions.

WORK–STRESS

Do you find your job awful? This jar may help you to reveal a bit of stress and anxiety related to your workplace and collages

WHAT YOU NEED:

* Black salt to cleanse yourself and suck up the negative energy
* Lavender to calm yourself down
* Lemon balm to get rid of stress
* Chamomile is also another anti-stress flower

* Sage to protect yourself from the negativity at your job
* Purple candle wax and amethyst to project it all outward

WHAT'S NEXT:

1. Place all the ingredients in the jar.
2. Keep it in your uniform pocket and hold it when you are stressed.

YULE JAR FOR A PROSPEROUS YEAR

Yule is the time to think about the coming year and meditate on the things to change for the better.

WHAT YOU NEED:

* Pink Himalayan Salt for happiness, positive energies, and prosperity
* Chilli flakes to ward off unwanted energies
* Basil for prosperity, money, and luck
* Cinnamon for luck, success, and power
* Ginger for plans coming into fruition quickly
* Nutmeg for luck, and encouraging favorable decisions
* Acorn for strength, endurance, prosperity, and luck
* Cedarwood for healing, insight, wisdom, and clarity
* Dry orange for fortune, health, wealth, good luck, and peace
* Rosemary to attract healing energy
* Moonstone chips for inner growth, new beginnings, strength, and success
* Obsidian for determination, grounding, and stability
* Red wax for vitality, strength, and courage
* Eggshells for transformation, protection, and strength

WHAT'S NEXT:

1. Cleanse your jar, hold it, and envision what you would like to achieve in the coming year.
2. Gather the correspondence together, and layer them in the jar. As you add them, say aloud what you're adding to the jar and the purpose.
3. Seal it with red wax once you're happy with it.

Rituals, Tarots, and Candle Spells

A couple of the following spells are a bit more advanced; save it for when you will feel ready.

I hope they will help you in manifesting your dream life!

~

Full Moon Ritual

This can be a good cleansing and energizing ritual as a preparation for other magical full moon rituals you wish to do that night.

WHAT YOU NEED:

* Yellow or orange candle
* Orange and pine essential oils
* Yellow or orange carnation flowers or petals
* Thyme, ginger, cinnamon, and lemon/orange Peel
* Bath salts of your choice
* Red, yellow or orange stones like Citrine, Garnet, or Carnelian

WHAT'S NEXT:

1. Light a candle says this incantation (as loud or as quiet as you want).

   "Moon above,
   Full and bright,
   Grant me energy
   This magical night."

2. Start pouring warm water into your bathtub, visualize your energy rising with each drop. You can add any of the listed essential oils, herbs, or flowers. If you are afraid of them getting stuck in the drain, you can use a material sachet.

3. Sometimes I used to take a bath with Crystals. Some of them don't like prolonged contact with water or might contain toxic elements. Use them with caution and always do your research. Gemstones that are seven or above on Mohs Hardness Scale are generally ok to use in water. If you don't want to soak them, you can place them around you or just quickly dip them in the bath for some crystal essence!

Devine Feminine (Self–Care Ritual)

Perfect to use to rebalance one's inner divine feminine energy and for love, beauty, and self-care rituals. Take this time to be still and receive the enchantment of this ritual. Feel free to drift off into reflection works.

WHAT YOU NEED:

* Sea salt
* Coconut milk powder
* Dried roses
* Dried lemon balm
* Dried yerba Santa
* Dried catnip
* Bergamot essential oil
* Ylang-ylang
* Essential oil

WHAT'S NEXT:

1. Transform your daily bath into a spiritual ritual, where you can unwind and find yourself by adding the herbs and oils to the water.
2. Set the water temperature in your bathtub between 80 to 95°F (27 to 35°C). The temperature is very important because it has therapeutic effects and makes you feel calm while rapidly relaxing your muscles.
3. For the skin: this soak works to soothe and heal the skin of irritation and sensitivities. Brings relief to sore muscles and aches. Purifies the body of toxins and rids it of impurities. For the spirit: this soak draws in love, beauty, and attraction while promoting the powers of healing, success, prosperity, and purification.

Psychic Dream (Candle Spell)

With this dream bag, you will open yourself up to the secrets that the universe wants to whisper to you.

WHAT YOU NEED:

* 1 white candle
* Trinkets in the shape of stars
* Sandalwood incense
* Amethyst
* Selenite
* Blue Vervain
* Rosemary
* Mugwort
* Lavender
* Blue Lotus
* A blue sachet bag
* 1 needle
* Purple thread

WHAT'S NEXT:

1. Set up a temporary dream altar on a bedside table where you will place your white candle and the star-shaped trinkets.
2. Light the candle and the sandalwood incense as you put together your psychic dream bag.
3. In the dream bag, place your amethyst and selenite. Hold the bag and ask the crystals to improve your psychic ability and open your third eye. Add your blue vervain, rosemary, mugwort, lavender, and blue lotus to the bag.
4. Close and sew your bag with the needle and thread to ensure nothing escapes while you sleep.
5. Allow your candle and incense to burn out before you sleep. Don't sleep while they burn!
6. Sleep with your sachet bag, either in your bed or on the bedside table that acted as your temporary dream altar.

Attract Romance (Candle and Tarots Spells)

While you can't force someone to be attracted to you, you can cast a spell that helps you to be open to the energies of love and passion that are undoubtedly available to you at any given time. This spell reminds you of your own persuasive powers of seduction and attraction.

Perform this spell on a full moon.

WHAT YOU NEED:

* 2 red candles
* Tarot cards: The Empress, Ace of Wands
* And a card signifying your potential lover

WHAT'S NEXT:

1. Place your candles in alignment with two opposing cardinal directions of the north (earth) and south (fire), placing The Empress card in between them. The Empress signifies beauty and abundance, and you are positioning her to draw in the energies from the elements.

2. Light your candles, and state your intentions clearly:

   "Come my love, come to me. Feel my flame and hear my pleas."

3. As the candles burn, draw the Ace of Wands and place it to the west (water), pointing toward The Empress card. Meditate on the beauty and powerful attraction of The Empress, who here represents you, while the Ace of Wands enhances that magical power washing over you.

4. When you feel your power at its peak, place the card signifying your potential lover— whatever you have chosen from the tarot deck—to the east (air) so all of your energy flows toward your target.

5. When the candles have burned down, bury the wax remains under a sturdy tree, preferably an apple tree symbolizing love.

Rose Attraction Potion

This potion is ideal for attracting potential new suitors or admirers into your life. It involves easy-to-find herbs and tools that you likely already have in your home. A rose is the best flower to use in this recipe due to its association with love. Best performed on a Friday or during a waxing moon.

WHAT YOU NEED:

* Small pot
* 1 cup water
* 1 teaspoon dried rose petals
* 1 teaspoon dried hibiscus flowers
* 1 teaspoon dried lavender flowers
* Pinch of cinnamon
* Muslin cloth or strainer
* Cup for drinking

WHAT'S NEXT:

1. Cleanse your kitchen.
2. In a small pot, boil the water as you set your intentions.
3. Remove the pot from the heat. Place the rose petals, hibiscus, lavender, and cinnamon one at a time into the pot. As you do this, repeat the following words four times.

"Infuse, imbue, impart, immerse"

4. Slowly stir the mixture as you visualize the energy of attraction wrapping around the herbs in the pot. Allow the potion to steep for 10 minutes.
5. Strain the potion into a cup and drink.

New Apartment Ritual

Moving into a new house is exciting, but you may come into contact with old, stagnant, or negative energy. A blessing for your new home is important for you and anyone you live with. Use this purification spell in your home to hit the reset button. Best permormed in every room of your new house, on a Saturday or during a dark moon.

WHAT YOU NEED:
* Lighter or matches
* Smudge stick or incense
* Fire-safe bowl
* Besom or feather

WHAT'S NEXT:
1. Begin in a room at the center of your home.
2. Light a smudge stick and place it in a fire-safe bowl.
3. Cleanse and purify the room by walking clockwise around it, carrying the bowl. Let the smoke fill the room, using a besom or feather to spread it. Say,

"With this smoke, I clear this dwelling
and banish all that needs repelling."

4. Visualize old and negative energies leaving your home.
5. Repeat steps 3 and 4 in each room of your house, starting from the center of each room and working clockwise around the house.

Love Spell Ritual

WHAT YOU NEED:

Sage to cleanse and bless yourself and space. Other cleansing and blessing herbs can be used, such as sweetgrass

Pink candle or red candle to promote passion, romance, and joy. A white candle can also be used

Nail for carving into candle

Rose petals for softening a heart, stimulates sex drive and encourages passion.

Lavender brings peace, relaxation, joy, and healing

Jasmine to encourages friendship

Jasmine oil

Rose oil

Rose Quartz to calm the mind, enhances self-love, and helps heal past trauma dealing with the heart

Paper and pen

~

WHAT'S NEXT:

Cleanse and Bless Your Space

Before any love spell ritual, it is important to cleanse and bless your space to get rid of any negative energy that may be lingering. Cleansing is done in many ways, but for this ritual, we will do a sage cleansing.

Light the sage and allow the smoke to bless the room. While doing this, visualize a white light surrounding you, filling you with love, happiness, power, and strength. Make sure to keep a window open or the door to let the smoke flow.

Mentally or out loud, invite your higher self, spirit guides, ancestors, or any god or deity you wish into the space and ask to be filled with love and the energy needed to manifest the desires of your heart.

Express gratitude for the deliverance of what you are manifesting and finish with a few seconds of stillness and silence.

So set your intention, write down on paper what you desire. A powerful intention is clear and direct.

For the next six mornings, starting the following morning after the spell, read your written intention aloud. On the sixth morning after reading, toss your written intention into flowing water to send it in to the universe—river, lake, or even toilet!

Please understand that it's important not to focus on manifesting someone specific but the characteristics that attract you to said person!

Prepare the Candle

Your intention is set, so now it's time to prepare your candle.

With a pin, carve one word on the side of the candle that represents what you desire (peace, love, joy, partner, romance, whatever you want!).

Then apply three drops of both the rose and jasmine oil to the candle in an upward motion. Next, crush together the dried roses, blue lavender, and jasmine; apply the herbal mix to the candle and rub on the candle in an upward motion. The upward motion is to encourage your manifestation to come to you instead of away from you.

"I straightforward invite you to this worldly connection of god and their function for the procedures of performing magical rites. I ensure you with the best voodoo and love spell which will embody magical powers."

Perform Love Spell Ritual

Start by lighting your candle. Then, hold on to your rose quartz with your right hand and imagine a pink light of warm love radiating from the rose quartz and engulfing you. The rose quartz exemplifies love energy.

Next, speak the incantation below with certainty and power:

Dancing flame that burns bright, I am love; it is my right. I choose to align with my desires of love, and thank you for the expedite! Appreciations I send throughout the night!

Candle Meditation

While the candle is burning, it is important to use that time to meditate and focus on desires. You can do this while focusing on the flame of the candle or with your eyes closed.

If you don't have time to sit and meditate, it is fine to snuff out the flame and come back later, but remember, it is crucial to finish burning the candle completely.

Closing of Love Spell

To finish out all spells or manifestations, it's critical to show gratitude to your higher-self, spirit guides, God or deity, or ancestors you invited into your space to assist with your manifestation. Speak as if your love spell has already come to fruition.

It is also important to reground yourself after a powerful love spell ritual; it can drain your energy. You can be reground by simply walking barefoot on the grass or dirt, drinking water, or even taking a few deep breaths.

After I perform a ritual, I write it down to keep a record of it and keep track of how long it takes for my manifestations to be fulfilled, and I suggest you do the same!

For the next six mornings, starting the following morning after the spell, read your written intention aloud. On the sixth morning after reading, toss your written intention into flowing water to send it in to the universe—river, lake, or even toilet!

Part 4

AT A GLANCE

"To each his own magic." — Libba Bray

INCENSE

Incense is good for amplifying spells or rituals and cleansing your area; plus, they smell really good! The list below is my personal reference sheet, straight out from my grimoire.

African Violet: Protection, spirituality. Creates and attract harmony in love

Allspice: Money, fortune and luck

Almond: Wisdom and prosperity

Aloes. Wood: Healing protection and affection

Amber: Healing, comfort and meditation. It is an emotional balancer!

Angelica: Protection, harmony and understanding, inspiration and meditation

Anise: Used for cleansing. It guides good luck charms, psychic pendulums and drives away negativity

Apple: Enhances wisdom and knowledge, healing, immortality and love

Bamboo: Divination, protection, luck and it is used for hex-breaking

Basil: Mental clarity, concentration and trust. Confidence, luck and love

Carnation: healing, protection and strength

Cedar. Wood: Used for purification, protection and for banishing bad dreams

Cherry: Money and relaxation

Cinnamon: Lust, healing, enhancing passion, psychic powers and attracts money powers

Clove: Attracts positive energies and enhances banishing rituals

Dragon's Blood: Used for exorcisms, it enhances love and protection

Eucalyptus: Used in healing rituals for protection and good health

Frankincense: Protection, purification, knowledge, meditation, spiritual growth and astral strength

Ginger. Root: Promote success and psychic growth

Hibiscus: Used in attraction rituals. Divination, lust and love

Honeysuckle: Enhance the bonds of love and heal relationships

Jasmine: Dream and relaxation. It may create prophetic dreams if burned in the bedroom

Juniper: Healing and purification from hexes

Lavender: Healing, cleanse your spirit, love and compassion

Lemongrass: Enhance psychic awareness

Lilac: Peace, harmony and protection

Lotus: Used in sacred offering and help with finding inner peace, fortune, love and long life

Nutmeg: Luck, prosperity and fertility

Orange: Money, luck and divination

Patchouli: Luck, love, prosperity and fertility

Peppermint: Renewal and growth

Pine: Health, protection and humility

Rosemary: Enhance memory and healing

Roses: Promote calm, love and healing

Sage: Wisdom and purification. It protects objects, home, and people

Sandalwood: Spiritual awareness and meditation. It is a psychic booster!

Sweetgrass: Purify spaces and attracts positive influences

Vanilla: Dedication and prosperity

Violet: Healing, purification, wisdom and luck

Flowers and Herbs

I love incorporating medicinal proprieties of herbs into my life too! If you were interested in the medical side of herbs and natural remedies for common ailments, I would recommend a book by a dear friend of mine, Tamaya Kawisenhawe. The best selling book ***Herbal Apothecary*** includes two manuscripts, and it is a fantastic guide for beginners! You can find it on Amazon.

Here, a list of 370 herbs and their spiritual proprieties to help you incorporate them into your magic.

Acacia: Protection and psychic powers. Love and money spells

Adam and Eve Roots: Happiness and love

Adders Tongue: Healing

Agaric: Fertility

Agrimony: Protection and sleep

Ague Root: Protection

Alfalfa: Money and prosperity, anti-hunger

Alkanet: Prosperity and purification

Allspice: Healing, money and luck

Almond: Wisdom, money and prosperity

Aloe: Protection and luck

Althea: Psychic powers and protection

Alyssum: It moderates anger

Amaranth: It heal heartbreak and create protection. Invisibly

Anemone: Healing, health and protection

Angelica: Used in exorcism, protection, healing, visions

Anise: Protection, youth and purification

Apple: Love, healing, immortality. Used in garden magic

Apricot: Love

Arabic Gum: Spirituality, purify negativity and protect from evil

Arbutus: Used in exorcism, protection

Asafoetida: Used in exorcism, purification and protection

Ash: Used in sea rituals for protection, prosperity and health

Aspen: Eloquence. Proper anti-theft!

Aster: Love

Avens: Used in exorcism, purification and love

Avocado: Beauty, lust and love

Bachelor's Buttons: Love

Balm, Lemon: Love, healing and success

Balm of Gilead: Manifestation, healing, love and protection

Bamboo: Protection, wished and luck. Often used in hex-breaking

Banana: Prosperity, fertility and potency

Banyan: Happiness and luck

Barley: Protection, love and healing

Basil: Protection, love, wealth. Used in exorcism

Bay: Protection, strength, psychic powers, healing and purification

Bean: Protection, wart charming, reconciliation, potency, love. Often used in exorcism

Bedstraw, Fragrant: Love

Beech: Wishes

Beet: Love

Belladonna: Vision, astral projection *TOXIC

Benzoin: Prosperity and purification

Bergamot, Orange: Success and money

Be-Still: Luck

Betony. Wood: Love, purification, protection

Birch: Protection, purification and cleansing. Often used in exorcism

Bistort: Fertility and psychic powers

Bittersweet: healing and protection

Blackberry: Protection, healing and money

Bladderwrack: Protection, money and psychic powers. Used in sea and wind spells

Bleeding Heart: Love

Bloodroot: Protection, love and purification

Bluebell: Truth and luck

Blueberry: Protection

Blue flag: Money

Bodhi: Protection, fertility, wisdom, meditation

Boneset: Protection. Used in exorcism

Borage: Courage and psychic powers

Bracken Brazil Nut Briony: protection, image magic and money

Bromeliad: Money and protection

Broom: Protection, purification, divination. Used in wind spells

Buchu: psychic powers and prophetic dreams

Buckthorn: Protection, wishes and legal matters. Often used in exorcism

Cabbage: Luck

Cactus: Chastity and protection

Calamus: Luck, money, healing and protection

Camellia: Riches

Camphor: Divination, purity and health

Caper: Luck, potency, and lust

Caraway: Protection, mental powers, lust, and health. Anti-theft!

Cardamon: Love and lust

Carnation: Protection, healing and strength

Carob: health and protection

Carrot: Lush and fertility

Cascara Sagrada: Legal matters, protection and money

Cashew: Money

Castor: Protection

Catnip: Magic, love, happiness and beauty

Cat Tail: Lust

Cedar: Healing, purification, money, protection

Celandine: Protection, happiness, legal matters and escape

Celery: Lush, mental and psychic powers

Centaury: Snake removing

Chamomile: Purification, sleep, love and money

Cherry: Love and divination

Chestnut: Love

Chickweed: Fertility and love

Chicory: Invisibility, favors, frigidity. Obstacles remover!

Chili Pepper: Fidelity and love. Used in hex breaking

China Berry: change and luck

Chrysanthemum: Protection

Cinchona: Luck and protection

Cinnamon: Spirituality, protection, lush, love, success, healing, power and psychic powers

Cinquefoil: Protection, money, prophetic dreams and sleep

Cloth of Gold: Understand animal languages

Clove: Protection, love, money, exorcism

Daffodil: Luck, fertility and love

Daisy: luck and lust

Damiana: Love, passion and visions

Dandelion: Divination, calling spirits, wishes

Datura: Sleep and protection. Used in hex breaking

Deer's Tongue: Lust and psychic powers

Devils Bit: Exorcism, protection, love and lust

Devils shoestring: Protection, employment,

luck gambling and power

DILL: Money, protection, luck and lust

DITANY OF CRETE: Astral projection, manifestations

DOCK: Money, healing and fertility

DODDER: Love, divination and knot magic

DOGBANE: Love

DOGWOOD: Protection and wishes

DRAGONS BLOOD: Potency, love, protection and used in exorcism

DULSE: Harmony and lust

DUTCHMAN'S BREECHES: Love

EBONY: Power and protection

ECHINACEA: Strengthening spells

EDELWEISS: Bullet-proofing and invisibility

ELDER: Protection, healing, sleep, prosperity. Exorcism

ELECAMPANE: Psychic powers, love, protection

ELM: Love

ENDIVE: Love and lust

ERYNGO: Peace, love, lust and traveler's luck

EUCALYPTUS: Protection and healing

EUPHORBIA: purification and protection

EYEBRIGHT: Mental and psychic powers

FENNEL: Protection, purification and healing

FENUGREEK: Money

FERN: Protection, luck, health, riches, eternal youth and rainmaking. Used in exorcism

FEVERFEW: Protection

FIG: Fertility, love and divination

FIGWORT: Health and protection

FLAX: Healing, protection, money, beauty and psychic powers

FLEABANE: Protection and chastity. Used in exorcism

FOXGLOVE: Protection

FRANKINCENSE: Protection and spirituality. Used in exorcism

FUMITORY: Exorcism and money

FUZZY WEED: Hunting and love

GALANGAL: Protection, money, lust, health and psychic powers. Used in hex-breaking

GARDENIA: Peace, healing love and spirituality

GARLIC: Protection, lush, healing, anti-theft and exorcism

GENTIAN: Power and love

GERANIUM: Fertility, love, health and protection

GIANT VETCH: Fidelity

GINGER: Money, success, love and power

GINSENG: Love, healing, protection, wishes, beauty and lust

GOATS RUE: Health and healing

GOLDENROD: Divination and money

GOLDEN SEAL: Money and healing

GORSE: Money and protection

GOTU KOLA: Meditation

GOURD: Protection

GRAIN: Protection

GRAINS OF PARADISE: Luck, love, wishes, lust and money

GRAPE: Money, fertility and mental powers. Used in garden magic

GRASS: Protection and psychic powers

GROUND IVY: Divination

GROUNDSEL: Healing and health

HAWTHORN: Happiness, fertility, chastity. Used in fishing magic

HAZEL: Wishes, luck, fertility, anti-lightning and protection

HEATHER: Luck, protection and rain making

HELIOTROPE: Healing, prophetic dreams, wealth and invisibility. Used in exorcism

HELLEBORE, BLACK: Protection *TOXIC

HEMLOCK: Destroy sexual drive *TOXIC

HEMP: Healing, love, meditation and vision

HENBANE: Love attraction ✴TOXIC

HENNA: Healing

HIBISCUS: love, lust and divination

HICKORY: Legal matters

HIGH JOHN THE CONQUEROR: Happiness, love, money and success

HOLLY: Protection, luck, balance and anti-lightning. Used in dream magic

HONESTY: Repelling monsters and money

HONEYSUCKLE: Protection, money, psychic powers

HOPS: Sleeps and healing

HOREHOUND: Protection, mental powers. Used in exorcism

HORSE CHESTNUT: Money and healing

HORSERADISH: Purification and used in exorcism

HORSETAIL: Fertility and snake charming

HOUNDS TONGUE: Tying dog's tongues

HOUSELEEK: Protection, love and luck

HUCKLEBERRY: Protection and luck. Used in dream magic and hex breaking

HYACINTH: Love, protection and happiness

HYDRANGEA: Hex breaking

HYSSOP: Purification and protection

INDIAN PAINT BRUSH: Love

IRIS: Wisdom and purification

IRISH MOSS: Money, protection and luck

IVY: Healing and protection

JASMINE: Prophetic dreams, love and money

JOBS TEARS: Wishes, healing and luck

JOE–PYE WEED: Respect and love

JUNIPER: Protection, health, love and anti-theft. Exorcism

KAVA–KAVE: Visions, luck and protection

KNOTWEED: Health and binding

LADY'S MANTLE: Love

LADY'S SLIPPER: Protection

LARCH: Protection and anti-theft

LARKSPUR: Health and protection

LAVENDER: Love, peace, protection, longevity, sleep, virtue, happiness and purification

LEEK: Love and protection. Used in Exorcism

LEMON: Longevity, love, purification, friendship

LEMONGRASS: Repel snakes, psychic powers, lust

LEMON VERBENA: Love and purification

LETTUCE: Sleep, love, purity, protection, divination

LIQUORICE: Lust fidelity and love

LIFE EVERLASTING: Longevity, healing, health

LILAC: Protection and beauty. Used in exorcism

LILY: Protection, breaking love spells

LILY OF THE VALLEY: Mental powers, happiness

LIME: Protection, love and healing

LINDEN: Protection, love, luck, immortality, sleep

LIQUID AMBER: Protection

LIVERWORT: Protection

LIVERWORT: Love

LOOSESTRIFE: Protection and peace

LOTUS: Protection and lock-opening

LOVAGE: Love

LOVE SEED: Friendship and love

LUCKY HAND: Employment, travel, luck, money and protection

MACE: Psychic and mental powers

MAGUEY: Lust

MAGNOLIA: Fidelity

MAHOGANY. MOUNTAIN: Anti-lightning

MAIDENHAIR: Love and beauty

MALE FERN: Love and luck

MALLOW: Love, protection. Used in exorcism

MANDRAKE: Protection, health, money, love and fertility

MAPLE: Love, money and longevity

MARIGOLD: Protection, prophetic dreams, psychic powers, business and legal matters

Marjoram: Healing, love, protection, happiness, money and health

Master Wort: Protection, strength, courage

Mastic Lush. Psychic powers, manifestations

May Apple: Money

Meadow Rue: Divination

Meadowsweet: Happiness, peace, love, divination

Mesquite: Healing

Mimosa: Love, protection, purification and prophetic dreams

Mint: Protection, love, money, travel, luck and healing. Used in exorcism

Mistletoe: Protection, health, love, fertility and hunting. Used in exorcism

Molukka: Protection

Moonwort: Love and money

Moss: Luck and money

Mugwort: Strength, protection, healing, psychic powers, prophetic dreams and astral projection

Mulberry: Protection and strength

Mullein: Courage, love, health, protection and divination. Used in exorcism

Mustard: Fertility, mental powers and protection

Myrrh: Protection, healing and spirituality. Exorcism

Myrtle: Love, money, peace, fertility and youth

Nettle: Lush, protection and healing. Used in exorcism

Norfolk Island Pine: Protection and anti-hunger

Nuts: Fertility, love, luck and prosperity

Oak: Protection, money, health, luck, healing, potency and fertility

Oats: Money

Olive: Healing, fertility, lush, peace, potency and protection

Onion: Protection, money, prophetic dreams, lust, healing and exorcism

Orange: Money, luck, love and divination

Orchid: Love

Oregon Grape: Money and prosperity

Orris. Root: Love, divination and protection

Palm. Date: Fertility and potency

Pansy: Love, divination and rain magic

Papaya: Love and protection

Papyrus: Protection

Parosela: Hunting

Parsley: Purification, love and protection

Passion Flower: Sleep, peace and friendship

Patchouli: Lush, money and fertility

Pea: Love and money

Peach: Love, wishes, fertility and longevity. Used in exorcism

Pear: Love and lust

Pecan: Money and employment

Pennyroyal: Strength, peace and protection

Peony: Protection and exorcism

Pepper: Protection and exorcism

Peppermint: Purification, love, sleep, healing and psychic powers

Pepper Tree: Purification, protection and healing

Periwinkle: Love, lust, money, protection and mental powers

Persimmon: Changing sex, luck and healing

Plot Weed: Protection

Pimento: Love

Pimpernel: Health and protection

Pine: Money, healing, fertility, protection. Used in exorcism

Pineapple: Chastity, money and luck

Pipsissewa: Money and spirit calling

Quassia: Love

Quince: Love, protection and happiness

Radish: Lush and protection

Ragweed: Courage

Ragwort: Protection

Raspberry: Protection and love

Rattlesnake Root: Money and protection

Rhubarb: Protection and fidelity

Rice: Rain, protection, fertility and money

Roots: Power, protection and divination

Rose: Love, psychic powers, luck, protection, healing and divination

Rosemary: Love, lust, mental powers, purification, protection, healing, sleep, youth. Used in exorcism

Rowan: Psychic powers, healing, protection, success and power

Rue: Healing, health, mental powers, love. Used in exorcism

Rye: Fidelity and love

Saffron: Love, lust, happiness, healing, wind raising, strength and psychic powers

Sage: Wish, wisdom, immortality, longevity and protection

Sagebrush: Purification and exorcism

St. Johns Wort: Love, happiness, health, power, protection, strength and divination

Sandalwood: Protection, healing, spirituality. Used in exorcism

Sarsaparilla: Money and love

Sassafras: Health and money

Summer Summer: Mental powers

Skullcap: Peace, love and fidelity

Senna: Love

Sesame: Money and lust

Shallot: Purification

Skunk Cabbage: Legal matters

Slippery Elm: Halts gossip

Sloe: Protection and exorcism

Snakeroot: Luck and money

Snakeroot/Black: Money, love and lust

Snapdragon: Protection

Solomons Seal: Protection and exorcism

Sorrel, Wood: Healing and health

Southern, Wood: Protection, love and lust

Spanish moss: Protection

Spearmint: Healing, love and mental powers

Spiderwort: Love

Spikenard: Love

Squill: Money and protection. Used in hex breaking

Star Anise: Psychic powers and luck

Stillengia: Psychic powers

Straw: Luck and image magic

Strawberry: Love and luck

Sugar Cane: Lush and love

Sumbul: Love, health, luck and psychic powers

Sunflower: Health, fertility, wishes, wisdom

Sweetgrass: Calling spirits

Tamarind: Love

Tamarisk: Exorcism and protection

Tansy: Health and longevity

Tea: Riches, strength and courage

Thistle: Strength, protection and healing. Used in hex breaking

Thistle Holy: Purification, used in hex breaking

Thistle Milk: Snake enraging

Thyme: Health, healing, love, sleep, psychic powers, courage and purification

Toadflax: Protection. Used in hex breaking

Toadstool: Rain making

Tobacco: Purification and healing

TURMERIC: Purification

TURNIP: Protection and ending relationships

URVA URSA: Psychic workings

VALERIAN: Sleeps, protection, love, purification

VANILLA: Lush, love and mental powers

VENUS FLYTRAP: Love and protection

VAPER: Luck, potency and lust

VARAWY: Protection, mental powers, lust and health. Anti-theft!

VERVAIN: Peace, love, protection, healing, purification, sleep, peace, money and youth chastity

VETIVER: Love, luck, money and anti-theft. Used in hex breaking

VIOLET: Protection, peace, love, lush, luck, healing and wishes

WAHOO: Courage, success. Used in hex-breaking

WALNUT: Health, mental powers, wishes and infertility

WAX PLANT: Protection

WHEAT: Money and fertility

WILLOW: Healing, divination, love, protection

WINTERGREEN: Protection and healing. Used in hex breaking

WINTERS BARK: Success

WITCH GRASS: Happiness, love, and lust. Used in exorcism

WITCH HAZEL: Protection and chastity Wolfs BANE: Protection and invisibility

WOOD ROSE: Luck

WOODRUFF: Victory, money and protection

WORMWOOD: Psychic powers, protection, love and calling spirits

YARROW: Courage, love, psychic powers. Used in exorcism

YELLOW EVENING PRIMROSE: Hunting

YERBA MATE: Love, fidelity and lust

YERBA SANTA: Beauty, psychic powers, healing and protection

YEW: Raising the dead

YOHIMBE: Love and lust

YUGGA: Purification, transmutation and protection

FLOWERS FOR THE LOVED ONES THAT PASSED

BEGONIA: Cordiality

CHRYSANTHEMUM: Life completion and sincerity

CROWN OF THORNS: Immortality, sacrifice, protection and faith

HYACINTH: Deep sadness

LILY OF THE VALLEY: Sweetness, purity and comeback of happiness

LIZ FLOWER: Honor and loyalty

MARIGOLD: Eternity, long life and peace

ROSES: Passion, love and romance

SNAPDRAGON (RED): Protection for your loved one, romantic love

SNAPDRAGON (WHITE): Peace and Protection

SUNFLOWER: Glory, dignity and passion jects, home, and people

SANDALWOOD: Spiritual awareness and meditation. It is a psychic booster!

SWEETGRASS: Purify spaces and attracts positive influences

VANILLA: Dedication and prosperity

VIOLET: Healing, purification, wisdom and luck

CRYSTALS

This is a list of crystals that have multiple uses. They are commonly known and generally easy to get a hold of.

If you're unsure if you can place your crystals in water and salt because it might damage the stone, use moonlight or starlight instead (on a full moon night). You can also pass your crystals through incense smoke or place them in a dry bath of herbs and flowers.

AGATE: Good luck, protection, strength, balance and inspiration

AMETHYST: Calming, balance, inner strength, emotional stability and protection from psychic attacks

AVENTURINE: Peace, happiness, prosperity and healing

CALCITE: Calming, reduce stress, amplifies energy, emotional healing, cleansing and memory

CARNELIAN: Manifestation, luck, creativity and protection

CITRINE: Creativity and motivation. It doesn't needs to be cleansed because it does not retain negative energy

CLEAR QUARTZ: Healing, power, protection, banishing and charging. It is a power stone used to provide extra energy and can be used to charge other items

FLUORITE: Peace and calm, stability, self-love, responsibility, impartial reasoning, meditation, concentration, protection from psychic attacks

HEMATITE: Deflecting negative energy and grounding

JASPER: Tranquillity, relaxation and protection

JET: Banishment, eases grief and protection

KYANITE: Removing energy blockages, cleansing other stones, tranquillity and channelling energy. It is a power stone used to provide extra energy and can be used to charge other items.

LABRADORITE: Dreams, reduce anxiety and stress, attract success, transformation, spiritual connection, peace and clarity

MILKY QUARTZ: Calming, luck, purification, soothing and meditation

OBSIDIAN: Grounding and transmuting negative energy

ONYX: Grounding

ROSE QUARTZ: Self-love, romantic love, calming and friendship

SELENITE: Mental clarity, cleansing and charging other crystals, removing energy blockages

SMOKY QUARTZ: Grounding, cleansing, banishing and removing emotional blockages

TIGER'S EYE: Self-discipline, protection, practicality, clarity, calmness, grounding, peace, intelligence, intuition and financial stability

DAY CORRESPONDENCE

In many magical traditions, the days of the week are crucial aspects for effective spellcasting. For example, you might prefer to work on a Wednesday for spell concerning business or communication due to the day's associations. While spells to do with abundance or prosperity could be done on Thursday because they are associated with riches and desire.

Not all traditions follow this rule. However, when you're doing any spellcasting, it is good to gather information about the best day of the week to make your magic happen. You going to be surprised to see some strong connections!

SUNDAY

PLANET: Sun

CORRESPONDENCES: Exorcism, healing, and prosperity

COLORS: Orange, white, and yellow

INCENSE: Frankincense and lemon

MONDAY

PLANET: Moon

CORRESPONDENCES: Agriculture, animals, female fertility, messages, reconciliation, and voyages

COLORS: Silver, white, and gray

INCENSE: African violet, honeysuckle, myrtle, willow, and wormwood

TUESDAY

PLANET: Mars

CORRESPONDENCES: Breaking negative spells, courage, military honors, physical strength, revenge, and surgery

COLORS: Orange and red

INCENSE: Dragon's Blood and patchouli

WEDNESDAY

PLANET: Mercury

CORRESPONDENCES: Business transactions, communication, divination, knowledge, and writing

COLORS: Grey, violet, yellow, all opalescent hues

INCENSE: Jasmine, lavender, and sweet pea

THURSDAY

PLANET: Jupiter

CORRESPONDENCES: Employment, happiness, health, luck, legal matters, male fertility, treasure, and wealth

COLORS: Indigo and purple

INCENSE: Cinnamon, musk, nutmeg, and sage

FRIDAY

PLANET: Venus

CORRESPONDENCES: Friendship, love, marriage, partnership, physical beauty, romance, and sexual matters

COLORS: Aqua, chartreuse, green, and pink

INCENSE: Rose, saffron, sandalwood, strawberry, and vanilla

SATURDAY

PLANET: Saturn

CORRESPONDENCES: Communication, locating lost or missing person, meditation, psychic attack or defense, and spirit

COLORS: Black, grey, and indigo

INCENSE: Myrrh and poppy seeds

Color Correspondence

The associations/correspondences of colors are fascinating. Color magic is a part of many traditions, and their associations are embedded in the collective consciousness.

When it comes actually to using these correspondences, be creative! It is a good idea to keep a variety of colored paper, cloths, fabric and ribbons, candles, or even ink on hand to use in different magical workings. You can incorporate herbs, flowers, or stones in the color of your choosing. You can write incantations and spells in the appropriate color, or use the corresponding color paper. If you do any Chaka work or meditate work, you can even visualize your aurea in the chosen color for your magic.

White: Truth, peace, purity, cleansing, spirituality

Pink: healing, love, harmony, romance, friendship

Purple: Spirituality, wisdom, power, psychic

Red: Passion, fire, love, strength, courage.

Brown: Earth, home, animals, stability, grounding

Green: Growth, luck, money, prosperity, abundance.

Yellow: Air, solar, learning, happiness, confidence.

Blue: Truth, water, peace, protection, healing

Gray: Contemplation, tarot, glamour, loneliness, negative

Silver: Moon, meditation, dreams, psychic, intuition

Gold: Energy, fortune, health, sun, success

Orange: Success, ambition, vitality, energy, creativity.

Black: Protection, death, binding, banishing, negativity.

Candle Substitutes

Candles are often among the things you need when casting a spell. However, you do not always have one on hand. Right? So, I created a short paragraph on how you can substitute the power of a candle!

Color: The color of the candle add meaning to your spell and helps solidify your intent. Instead of a candle, you can use other colored objects to represent the same meaning.

Smell: The oils and herbs used in candles give particular scents that you may use to your advantage. As a replacement, you can use naturally scented soaps or oils and herbs themselves.

Fire: When you burn a candle, energy is released into the space, and this process can empower your spell. You can release energy in other ways to replace this aspect. For example, physically moving, dancing, or exercising releases the energy stored in your body.

Warmth: Heat is a form of energy that is easily felt and transferred through candles. If your spell requires a heat source, consider investing in a wax melter. These will release heat in addition to having significance in color and smell!

Light: It is common to light candles for the dead because the power of the light lies in helping the spirits find their way through our realm. If what you need is light, you could consider a lightbulb!

Symbolism: Other times, the power of a candle lies in the image of the candle itself. Consider different representations, or you can find apps that allow you to display a burning candle.

Honey Magic

Honey has been utilized by nearly every culture across the globe for food, healing, and spiritual purposes. And it is universally considered a talisman of beauty, health, prosperity, and sweetness. It is convenient as you can probably find it in your cupboard, and it can be utilized in different types of witchcraft.

Honey can be drizzled onto the earth, into a body of water or onto a candle and burned.

Because it is excellent at preserving itself, honey is extremely helpful to witches with long-term altars or forgetful ones - like me! It can be drizzled into an offering bowl and left on an altar for extended time without worries.

Healing: Honey has been used to treat wounds since the time of the Ancient Egyptians. Because it contains natural antibacterial properties, metaphysically, it can be added to protection spells or wards to create an environment of sterility and positivity. Honey can also be added to healing spells to strengthen the recovery process.

Sweetness: One of honey's most ancient uses, from Greek to Egyptian to Voudoo, is to add 'sweetness' to a spell. It can be used to make the effects more pleasant and inviting. For example, honey can be added to glamour magic to make the illusion more easily accepted; to curses to make the energy seem harmless when entering the target's life; to money or job spells to 'sweeten the deal; to love or sex spells to sweeten a relationship or conjure an appealing partner.

Offering: Since the time of the Ancient Egyptians, honey has always been used as an offering that symbolizes care, the utmost love, and respect. Its final use is beneficial to witches who work with fairies, the Dead, nature spirits or deities because it contains a very warm and pleasing energy that is enticing to spirits.

Beauty: On its own or added to face masks, it can moisturize, nourish and cleanse the skin. It can also be added to glamour and beauty spells to add a sweet glow to your energy.

Prosperity: Honey represents abundance and can be added to spells for abundance, wealth, fertility, or prosperity to amplify the effects and create a surplus in your life.

Witchy Recipes

~

Dragon Blood's Ink

I know it's an old craft, and in modern times witches no longer need to make their ¬inks, but...

Dragon blood ink is a great way to give your written spells a boost, and I think that natural inks are much more potent than modern synthetic alternatives. Remember that Dragon blood ink is for positive spell work; you need the bat blood version if you are cursing or hexing.

Resins: Dracaena cinnabari and Draceana Draco are suitable for creating ink as they quickly dissolve in alcohol. While Daemonorops draco is not alcohol soluble. If mixed with alcohol, this palm draco resin may turn the alcohol a muddy brown color, but will quickly settle to the bottom.

WHAT YOU NEED:

1 teaspoon Dragon's Blood Resin
1 teaspoon ground gum arabic
15 teaspoons alcohol

WHAT'S NEXT:

First, you have to powder the resin. I like to wrap the resin in baking paper and crush it using the pestle to minimize wastage.

Soak the powdered resin in the alcohol and watch the blood color seeping into the liquid and transforming into a rich, black-red fluid.

Leave it in a warm, dry place and allow the alcohol to evaporate.

Add the gum.

Filter through a cloth, leaving the bark chunks behind.

Use a brush to make some tests to obtain the correct concentration. If it becomes too thick, add more alcohol and let it evaporate again.

Store in a dark bottle.

Black Salt

Black salt is very easy to do at home. It is basic stuff in witchcraft. It may be used to make a salt circle (instead of regular white salt), break bad spells (hexes), and banishing.

You may want to use black salt in various rituals too. Some blogs recommend adding food coloring to the salt. But salt gets clumpy and then dissolves when in contact with a liquid. So, it is better to use something dry to color it! For example, you could use fine ash from your fire or, or black chalk dust or, scrapings from a cast-iron skillet or, finely ground black pepper

You may have to slightly adjust the portions a little, depending on the density of your coloring ingredient. But here is a basic recipe for making it:

2 parts sea salt + 1-part dry black coloring

TIPS:

Black salt should be stored in an airtight jar.

Add essential oil for an added boost.

Instead of pouring salt everywhere for cleansing and protection, try misting saltwater from a spray bottle! The salt is unnoticeable to guests, and there is no gritty clean-up!

~

Egg Shell Powder

Egg shells powder is essential in witchcraft because it purifies and protects.

Among its powers, eggs shells block negative energies, so it is excellent for when you want to sit, meditate and center for a little while. You can also sprinkle it across your doors or windows or even use it to draw sigils or seal bottle spells. Egg shells can be used to protect spiritual beings from the physical space. You can use it to enhance your psychic abilities by rubbing a little on your skin - it will also protect you from what seeks to take advantage of you. Another use is in baths for purification purposes; adding it to the water will increase the cleansing effect. You can even share it with your plants as it makes great plant food. I also add it to my homemade pet food as a calcium supplement!

IT IS SO EASY TO MAKE. ALL YOU HAVE TO DO IS:

Boil empty eggs shells for 10 minutes.

Drain the water and place the shells on a paper towel to dry overnight.

Place the egg shells in a placement paper and bake them for about 10 minutes at 200 degrees (F) – make sure they are completely dried!

When they are cool enough to handle, finely ground them. Ideally, you want to use a coffee grounder, but a kitchen mixer will do the job.

Store it away from sunlight, moisture, and heat in an airtight container.

Conclusions

Jar/bottle spells (or Witch Spells) are a time-honored tradition in witchcraft and folk magic and are a versatile and powerful form of spell work. If mastered, they can help you to achieve success with real-world results, such as attaining love, getting rid of unwanted situations, or getting a pay rise at your work.

Do not get discouraged if your spells do not work at first; every witch has to fail to learn and develop her powers and magic skills. Just keep trying and adjusting. Have faith; with time, you will feel more powerful in your practice, further your spirituality, and be able to craft your destiny.

Before saying bye, I would like to share what I wish someone had told me when I first started.

Have a special shawl, scarf, or headcover - This helps you block out light and activate your inner vision more efficiently, allowing you to enter trance faster. Especially if you have trouble concentrating. And, if you enchant it to do so, it may hide your energy from harmful spirits.

If you have the ability, smoke it! - Herbal bundles, including white sage, may assist with aura protection, awakening your senses, entering meditation, and supporting your energy work. Some are also effective in warding off evil spirits! However, be cautious while using essential oils, fragrances, and incenses; not all of them are safe to use externally, internally, or at all times. Do your research before!

Believe in your guides, protective spirits, angels, and higher self, among other things - It's virtually always for your advantage if they ask or tell you to do anything. Learn from my errors and use them to your advantage rather than against you. When you work with the Spirit World, you'll go farther and faster.

Recognize that it isn't all about you - Things may become difficult, and magic work may bring up a lot of self-work and shadow work that has to be released. Things begin to open once you allow them to. Keep in mind that things happen to you, not to you. Nothing can unsettle you when you claim and walk into your authority. Things may attempt to bring you down, and you always rise to the occasion. The journey is just as vital as the destination.

You'll never know everything - In fact, you probably don't know much at all. You won't know or experience everything else that everyone else has, so be cautious while being open and accepting. Deal with the fact that you will never know everything. Do not dismiss someone or what they are going through if their experience contradicts your ideas or what you believe is occurring. In any case, we all have various perspectives on things.

Don't overdo things - A little goes a long way. Respect your feelings of exhaustion and exhaustion by taking a break. Take a break for a bit. You can't and shouldn't expect to be able to channel or heal or do anything else constantly or back-to-back for the rest of your life. Allow yourself to set boundaries. I'm sure there's a lot more, but this is a decent start on what I wish someone had told me when I first started.

Bless you,

P.A.

Spells Index

~

Printed in the USA
CPSIA information can be obtained
at www.ICGtesting.com
LVHW010452031123
762898LV00007B/213

9 781802 850703